'Conquering England'
Ireland in Victorian London

'Conquering England'
Ireland in Victorian London

Fintan Cullen and R.F. Foster
Foreword by Fiona Shaw

National Portrait Gallery

Published in Great Britain by
National Portrait Gallery Publications
National Portrait Gallery
St Martin's Place
London WC2H 0HE

Published to accompany the exhibition 'Conquering England' Ireland in Victorian London
held at the National Portrait Gallery, London, from 9 March to 19 June 2005.

For a complete catalogue of current publications please write to the address above, or
visit our website at www.npg.org.uk/publications

ISBN 1 85514 348 8

A catalogue record for this book is available from the British Library.

Publishing Manager: Celia Joicey
Editor: Susie Foster
Copy Editor: Lesley Levene
Design: Price Watkins Design
Production: Ruth Müller-Wirth
Printed and bound in Hong Kong

Contents

Director's foreword

Relations between the Irish and the English have long been characterised by stereotypes of one kind or another. Maybe this is the case for all connections forged within a colonial context. And in the post-colonial and post-immigration era it may be more difficult to look back and understand the concepts and images that were available – some of which were fading and some emergent – by which Dublin might portray London and vice versa.

This exhibition explores portraiture and the arts as a crucial route by which metropolitan London could understand and admire the expansive creativity of Ireland in the nineteenth century. Certain simplified images may have influenced perceptions of the Irish: the poet, the political radical, the manual worker and the muse amongst them. But these visual stereotypes could only go so far. The bursting energy of figures ranging from Daniel O'Connell and Charles Stewart Parnell to Oscar Wilde, W.B. Yeats and George Bernard Shaw soon found wonderful expression in sketches and caricatures, as well as in full portraits.

Wilde claimed in the *Picture of Dorian Gray* that 'The moral life of man forms part of the subject-matter of the artist, but the morality of art consists in the perfect use of an imperfect medium.' Art may thus have its limits, but this book and the exhibition that it accompanies exploit art as the means to bring back to life the principal Irish protagonists from the nineteenth-century worlds of politics, literature and the theatre.

'Conquering England' has been conceived, developed and researched by Professors Fintan Cullen and Roy Foster. It follows the Gallery's publication of *The Irish Face* by Fintan Cullen in 2004. Whilst focusing on a narrower period, this book and exhibition bring complementary perspectives to the subject by reviewing a wider range of material. I am most grateful to both authors for the exceptional diligence that they have brought to the enterprise. I am also grateful to Peter Funnell, Curator of Nineteenth-century Portraits, and Sophie Clark, Exhibitions Manager, for guiding the collaboration, and to other Gallery staff including Pim Baxter, Naomi Conway, John Haywood, Ruth Kenny, Jude Simmons, Hazel Sutherland, Carol Trevor and Rosie Wilson. The book has been edited by Susie Foster, produced by Ruth Müller-Wirth and designed by Price Watkins, and I should like to thank them for their care and hard work. Grateful thanks also go to Fiona Shaw for her preface, and to the many lenders without whom the exhibition would not have been possible.

Sandy Nairne
Director
National Portrait Gallery, London

Foreword

In my father's dining room in Cork, there hangs a picture of neighbouring Cobh harbour by Richard Atkinson. Bunting is flying from a large ship and in a small boat a local dignitary is being rowed out to welcome the cause of the celebration, Queen Victoria. She arrived in Cobh in 1849, renamed it Queenstown and opened the university in Cork, which later, after Independence, buried her statue in the grounds … and which, even later, I attended.

As a small child, the view from the sitting-room window was the exact view of the painting: straight out to the harbour, with the famous gap between the headlands from where so many left the country during the Famine. More recently, Cobh was the last port of call for the *Titanic* before its maiden death, and from the harbour's mouth the bodies from the lost *Lusitania* were spat onto the shore. To my young eyes watching the *Inisfallen* ferry to Pembroke, it was the gateway to the cultural mecca of England. And down the road from our Cork dwelling allegedly was Kitty O'Shea's erstwhile home. She who had caused Parnell to fall. We passed it every day.

When I arrived as a student in London in 1980, I carried some of Ireland's artistic giants with me. They had been like rugby players, ambassadors for us smaller folk. I walked the streets of Oscar Wilde's Chelsea and Daniel Maclise's Westminster, I passed the bust of George Bernard Shaw every day as I ran between classes at RADA and, eventually, I even bought a flat on the same street as William Butler Yeats's house in Fitzroy Road. Unlike them, however, I was female and Catholic. I arrived at RADA in a tweed skirt and a Shetland sweater and sat awestruck by the 'hip' actors who were using pieces of Tom Stoppard and Harold Pinter as their calling cards – I was armed with an eighteenth-century Irishman, William Congreve.

There was a kind of raggy arrogance in London then. Punk was on the way out, humour was aggressive and modern drama quite violent. The culture had changed and I was unprepared and terrified. I quickly felt the different mores of the generation I was joining. I was not strong on chart music and, fresh from an Irish university, I was hot on religion and metaphysics, and so utterly uncool.

However, slowly I discovered there was a benefit in being from the 'other' island. My parochialism became exotic. People were interested in the details of my childhood that I had taken for granted. My relative innocence was a source of mirth, but Irish people have always been that and never minded. I was treated kindly, given wonderful invitations and so I struggled through, barely keeping up with the modern writers in the first years and only coming into my own when we hit anything before 1900. In the theatre it was Shakespeare that devastated me – the brilliant *Hamlet* of Jonathan Pryce, Harriet Walter at the Royal Court and *Othello* with Paul Scofield at the National Theatre. The English National Opera was a revelation, as was the National Gallery and its vast treasures. We had nothing like them in Ireland.

There was more poverty in London than I had expected. Pubs seemed to lack the charm of Irish bars as I began to peel away from my Irish safety net and trade on my sharpening differences. We Irish are not suburban and I wonder if that was not a strength of those who came a century before. The price of belonging to an empire is that your place is set, your position defined. The joy for the outsider is that you can be anything.

Oscar Wilde affected the room when he entered; so did Yeats, Parnell and Shaw. They were armed with the language of London, trained in its mandarin dialects, but they and I in my tiny way were not defined by its prescriptions. They were 'flamboyant with attitude' and tested the boundaries of the tolerance of the London they entered. These artists came because 'home' was too small for them and London, with its great addictive charm and size, was in turn shrunk into a Dublin by their swagger and anarchy. But they, too, were conquered, Shaw living his whole long life there, Yeats staying a considerable time (despite wishing to go to Innisfree) and Wilde tragically crumbling under the weight of its establishment's wrath. It takes a lot of energy to break through the carapace of another culture, but once you have, you find the skin has closed behind you.

The Ireland that I grew up in was not that different from that of the late nineteenth century and was as if slowly waking from a dream. We had been 'caught in that sensual music'. Neutrality had numbed us (my grandmother called the War 'the Emergency'). We had a boastful tradition of exporting writing but we had an isolation that meant that until the magic kiss of the 'green tiger', we continued much as we had the previous century. Ireland seemed nearly outside time, but that timelessness had allowed its inhabitants to breathe to a different rhythm, to take time to hear or tell as Yeats put it, '… a mocking tale or a gibe/To please a companion/Around the fire at the club'. Wilde, Shaw, Yeats and many of their contemporaries charmed their way with an eccentric confidence and refreshing opinion that named their individuality more than their national identity. They declared their genius with an ironic twist. There are signs of this trait still in today's resident Irish artists in London. Their presence in Britain gives inspiration to those who follow them from Ireland – rolling out a carpet on which newcomers can tread. I learned the English ways and, like my predecessors, used humour as my tool of entry, making my debut in the Irish playwright Sheridan's *The Rivals* at the National Theatre in 1983.

Recently, the university in Cork celebrated its 150-year anniversary by digging up the statue of Victoria, who had lain gently under the lawn of the President's garden since 1922. She now stands forgivingly in a display case. Perhaps she and we are finally learning that the conquering is mutual. For the visitor, to arrive is to be conquered too.

Fiona Shaw
August 2004

Curators' preface

England had conquered Ireland, so there was nothing for it but to come over and conquer England

George Bernard Shaw[1]

Under the Union between Great Britain and Ireland in 1801, the two countries were engaged in a relationship that was quarrelsome, contentious, and in many ways inter-dependent. Exploitative as the connection between the countries often was, it also provided a wider arena for certain ambitions, in literature, politics and the arts. Irish talent was exported to London in the nineteenth century; by the turn of the twentieth, it was being imported back, with interest, to an Ireland undergoing political radicalisation and cultural renaissance.

The reign of Victoria demarcates a convenient period in which to explore the contentious and contradictory relationship that existed between the two islands of Britain and Ireland. As well as being an era that consolidated the union of parliaments, it also witnessed the disestablishment of the Anglican Church of Ireland, and saw the Parnellite Irish Parliamentary Party come to hold the balance of power at Westminster in the mid-1880s. More tangibly, during this period London became the metropolis of the empire and the mecca to which all subjects were drawn. Irish politicians were obliged to attend Westminster, but the city also attracted Irish artists, writers, playwrights, actors, journalists and those seeking advancement in a wide range of human endeavour. This book – which is the product of an exhibition of the same name – explores the cultural and political diversity of the Irish presence in London. The focus is on the visual representation of the Irish. We discuss, for example, the hitherto unacknowledged presence of a group of Irishwomen models in the London art world of the later nineteenth century and highlight the London reaction to such events as the year-long hearings of the Special Commission on Parnellism and Crime in 1888–9, as sketched by Sydney Prior Hall. The high-focus self-promotion of figures such as Oscar Wilde, W. B. Yeats and George Bernard Shaw appears through a range of images produced for public consumption by either London-based photographers or through the pages of illustrated magazines such as the *Graphic*, the *Tatler* or the *Sketch*. At the very end of the period, with the Celtic craze and events such as the new Abbey Theatre's visits to London, Ireland had become 'fashionable'; it was at this point too that the focus of Irish cultural effort shifted back to Dublin, providing a logical closure.

In covering the period from the 1830s to the turn of the century, we move from art through politics to literature and drama, while establishing cross-connections between these various worlds. The Irish were prominent in other spheres also, notably medicine and the law: in 1894 an Irish-born Catholic, Charles Russell, became Lord Chief Justice of England after an immensely distinguished career at the Bar, combined with a political life spent supporting Home Rule at Westminster. But the worlds of the visual arts, politics, literature (both popular and highbrow) and the stage retain the most vivid impression of Irish influence in Victoria's reign. At the same time, in exploring the presence of the Irish in London, this study is not limited to artists of Irish origin. Some came to London from Ireland, such as Daniel Maclise and John Henry Foley, as well as John Lavery, John Butler Yeats and lesser-known figures such as John Doyle and Althea Gyles. Others, like Ford Madox Brown, Sydney Prior Hall, Julia Margaret Cameron and Aubrey Beardsley, were English, yet were interested in representing Irish people and events at the heart of empire. And others were neither Irish nor English: James McNeill Whistler was American, while David d'Angers was French.

In enlarging our choice of images when discussing the representation of Ireland, we have amassed a wide range of visual material which moves from objects exhibited at the highly respectable Royal Academy of Arts in London or the more progressive Grosvenor Gallery founded in 1877, to pages from popular magazines, book illustrations and theatre posters – ephemera which convey in retrospect a vital moment of cultural history. The original exhibition contained sculpture, paintings, drawings, engravings, photographs, theatre programmes and book covers, as well as manuscripts by such writers as Yeats and Wilde. The final aim of this book is to indicate the variety, achievement and impact of these artists in Victorian London.

In conclusion, the curators wish to acknowledge the following for all their help and support: Sally Brown, Claire Connolly, Nick Daly, Julie Donovan, Patrick Guinness, Richard Hawkins, Janice Helland, Anne Hodge, Michael Holroyd, Kenneth McConkey, Sheila O'Connell, Mark Pomeroy, Martin Postle, Marion Pringle, Roger Swift, Deirdre Toomey, Robert Towers and W.E. Vaughan. Sandy Nairne and the staff at the National Portrait Gallery have been admirably resourceful and supportive throughout, especially Peter Funnell, but also Sophie Clark and Rosie Wilson in the Exhibitions Department, and Susie Foster, Celia Joicey and Ruth Müller-Wirth in the Publications Department. We should also like to thank Charles Saumarez Smith, who originally commissioned the project. We are extremely grateful to all lenders to the show and to the individuals in various institutions who made the loans possible as well as supplying us with valuable information.

Fintan Cullen
R.F. Foster
September 2004

NOTE
1 Quoted in Holroyd, Vol. I (1988), p.60; originally quoted in Lady Keeble (Lillah McCarthy), 'Bernard Shaw as I knew him' (unpublished memoir, Columbia University).

'An Irish Power in London': making it in the Victorian metropolis

R.F. Foster

Among those people forgotten or excluded from mainstream history, and condemned to what E.P. Thompson called 'the immense condescension of posterity', some thought should be spared for the Irish middle class. Less immediately glamorous than Fenian revolutionaries or decayed Anglo-Irish ascendancy, less affecting than Land League agitators or heroic emigrants, they still deserve their place in the remarkable story of how Ireland, Irish tropes, Irish causes and Irish idioms stamped their mark on British consciousness during the imperial era. Until quite recently, one used to hear the unthinking assertion that nineteenth-century Ireland didn't have a middle class – an assertion easily disproved by one look at Irish fiction, not to mention provincial architecture, or the (admittedly limited) research that has been done on nineteenth-century material culture. Now historians are placing class, and class cultures, much nearer the centre of Irish social history in the nineteenth and early twentieth centuries. Part of this story should include the way that Irish people colonised central areas of London metropolitan life in the Victorian period – notably journalism, the law, medicine, the arts and, of course, politics. It is a subject which has relevance for the continuing debates about the images of the Irish prevalent in Victorian Britain: the question of ethnically derogatory generalisations, or cartoons that represent the Irish in simian form, for instance, and the arguments about segregationist or assimilationist patterns of social life.[1] Both these invigorating discussions tend to ignore the fact that not all Irish emigrants to Victorian Britain were working class (much as the activities of the Irish in the networks of imperial administration have just begun to be investigated); and also commentators have tended to ignore just how visible Irish people were in a range of high-profile professions and projects, often generating an impressive level of publicity through the London-based media.

Moreover, in many cases what they were involved in marketing or publicising concerned views or interpretations of Ireland, contemporary or historical. This reached a climax at the end of Victoria's reign and the beginning of the twentieth century. But the work presented here suggests that the astonishing impact of the Celtic revival and the Irish cultural renaissance from the 1890s both builds upon and has affinities with the enterprise of earlier Irish cultural entrepreneurs in the Victorian capital who were, like W.B. Yeats and his friends, working against a political background where Irish matters were a continual presence and Irish voices a distinct part of the UK chorus. The concept of 'Victorian Ireland' has come into historiographical focus over the last twenty years or so.[2] But there is another way too in which

George Bernard Shaw, 1856–1950

Sir Bernard Partridge, 1894
Watercolour on board,
267 x 184mm
(10½ x 7¼")
National Portrait Gallery,
London (NPG 4229)

An actor and a caricaturist, Partridge was later to become a chief cartoonist for *Punch*. There is a touch of caricature in this lively portrait of GBS, who is shown, script in hand, at a rehearsal of his first great success, *Arms and the Man*. Partridge (under his stage name of Bernard Gould) played Sergius in the first production. Four days after the play's opening, the drawing was reproduced in the *Sketch* (Vol.5), a new London journal of the 1890s, set up to focus on 'Art and Actuality'.

Ireland is at the centre of Victorian Britain – and not just in the sense of building roads, working in factories and digging canals, vital though this contribution was. London was the magnet for generations of middle-class Irish *arrivistes* determined to make their mark. As George Bernard Shaw put it, 'Every Irishman who felt that his business in life was on the higher planes of the cultural professions felt that he must have a metropolitan domicile and an international culture; that is, he felt his first business was to get out of Ireland.'[3] And he knew what he was talking about.

These ideas are illustrated here by the rich harvest of images to be gleaned from the National Portrait Gallery in London and other collections, depicting the integration of a prominent Irish presence in the worlds of art, literature, intellectual life and politics – as well as showing the kind of images of Ireland produced in London and displayed for a metropolitan audience, from the early years of Victoria's reign up to the very early twentieth century. The shift in imagery is symbolised by two striking paintings, Daniel Maclise's *The Origin of the Harp* of 1842 (see p.58) and John Butler Yeats's portrait of his son William Butler Yeats, painted around 1900 (see p.17). Both were done in London by Irish painters who had come there to make their careers and both present iconic images of Irish culture. Both are in a sense romanticised, but the very different styles chart the distance travelled from the florid romanticism of the early nineteenth century to the dramatic simplicity of the Yeats portrait. Yet there are connections. The Maclise represents an earlier era when Irish poetry had conquered an influential metropolitan audience, just as Yeats did in the 1890s, since it depicts the immensely popular Irish poet Thomas Moore's lyric of the same name, dealing with national origins, suffering and deliverance, as well as creating one of the most enduring feminised images of Erin. Maclise would follow this through in another national depiction, where he portrays the Irish writer Caroline Norton as Erin – once again in full-blown goddess mode (see p.68). Caroline Norton, of course, also stands for another theme: the Irish influence in nineteenth-century London journalism. The model for George Meredith's novel *Diana of the Crossways* (1885), she was a well-connected Irishwoman who left a disastrous marriage to pursue a career as a political commentator and contributor to some of the most influential journals of the day (among other achievements, she leaked the news of the repeal of the Corn Laws to *The Times*). As Meredith's novel stressed, her Irish identity was central to her image as a dangerous wit, with an air of scandal about her, who was able to slip through some of the boundaries imposed on intellectual women in mid-Victorian Britain.

Though Norton is not usually grouped with the Irish writers who colonised whole areas of the journalistic world, she should be. By 1872, Hugh Heinrick's survey of the Irish in England could point out that the Irish influx into London comprised people of all classes who, combined,

constitute an Irish power in London which in point of intellect, patriotic earnestness, energetic manhood and fidelity to faith and fatherland, are not excelled by any section of the Irish people on earth ... [Irish intellect] dominates in the studios, shines in the closet, and educates and rules in the press ... There is not a newspaper in London without its one, two, three and four Irish writers and Irish reporters on its staff – indeed, Irish reporters are not alone numerous, but are the best and ablest who supply the daily papers with the Court and Parliamentary records of the day.[4]

Heinrick has a tendency to hyperbole, but here he can give chapter and verse; and his point about parliamentary reporting being in the hands of the Irish is important, as is his later remark that the sub-editors on London papers tend to run an Irish monopoly too. Frank Hugh O'Donnell would later recall that by 1870 the Tory *Morning Post* was run by Irish nationalists in all its key departments; by 1890 *The Times's* parliamentary correspondent was yet another Irish Home Ruler.[5] Indeed, Irish influence was pervasive throughout the provincial press of the whole island.[6] Heinrick makes the point that Irish journalists aren't above tailoring their opinions to Saxon values (if the price is right), but as an early Home Ruler he saw the importance of a sympathetic print media. This, of course, was spotted by Daniel O'Connell when he moved from being the 'Liberator' who delivered political emancipation to Catholics in 1829 to becoming the chief of the Irish political machine at Westminster, seeking repeal of the Act of Union in the 1830s. There could be an entire exhibition on images of O'Connell, many of them generated in London for a London market; his position as an insider comes clearly across in John Doyle's striking sketch, significantly called *A Family Group* (see p.40). O'Connell stands behind the windows of Brooks's Club, with two Irish political allies, Ebrington and Duncannon.[7] Indeed, one of the most celebrated full-size portraits of O'Connell has long adorned the front lobby of the Reform Club.

While O'Connell had his circles of Irish media influence, not all influential Irish writers in early Victorian London were nationalists (John Wilson Croker comes to mind); the circle around *Fraser's Magazine*, however, brought in a wide range of opinions and provided, for instance, William Makepeace Thackeray with much of the material he used for his portrait of the Irish journalistic subculture in his novel *Pendennis*, featuring a whole gallery of Irish newspapermen, like the interchangeable Mr Hoolan and Mr Doolan of *The Dawn* and *The Day*. (His portrait of the Irish editor Shannon, who managed things from Boulogne because of his bailiffs, was clearly based on yet another *arriviste* Irish writer, Charles Lever.) William Maginn, the powerful editor of *Fraser's*, was a Corkman; Maclise's drawing of *The Fraserians* (see p.27), for the 'Gallery of Illustrious Literary Characters' published in the magazine in 1835, includes Francis Sylvester Mahony, Thomas Crofton Croker and Francis Stack Murphy with Thomas Carlyle and Thackeray (both of whose commentaries on Ireland were to be influential in very different ways). Both Maclise and the sculptor John Henry Foley were (as Heinrick also pointed out) immensely influential creators of the iconography of British Victorian identity, through works for great public display, such as Maclise's richly referential history murals for the walls of the House of Lords, or Foley's massive group representing Asia for the Albert Memorial.

The interlocking worlds of professional Irish writers and artists in London from Victoria's accession must be seen against the background of recurrent political crisis in Ireland, and the uneven attempts of the British government and administration to deal with them. Through the 1830s and early 1840s a series of commissions and inquiries and attempted political initiatives tried ineffectively to grapple with Irish poverty, Irish religious affairs and Irish education, though none could obscure the clear fact that the Union was operating as 'a partnership of loss'. All this was thrown into starker relief than ever by the horrors of the Great Famine, which devastated Ireland from the mid-1840s. The images of Irish famine in the *Illustrated London News* have been much discussed, and the point has been made that they represent, if anything, a prettified representation of horror. While the amount of space devoted to them is nonetheless striking, more elaborate visual images of the Famine are few; they tend to emerge in the form of genre paintings over the next few years. Painters like George Frederic Watts and Erskine Nicol depicted scenes of starvation and eviction in works that were exhibited and discussed in London – none more so than the Irish painter Robert Kelly's *An Ejectment in Ireland (A Tear and a Prayer for Erin)* (see p.70), exhibited in 1853 and allegedly the subject of discussion in the House of Commons.[8] (This theme continued, culminating in Lady Butler's painting of an eviction, displayed in 1890, which drew a famously brutal reaction from Lord Salisbury: in a speech at the Royal Academy of Arts he enthusiastically commended the '"breezy beauty" of the landscape, which almost made him wish he could take part in an eviction himself'.)[9]

Irish images continued a dominant presence in illustrated magazines, and have been the subject of much discussion by historians since Perry Curtis first advanced his thesis connecting English and American cartoonists' depictions of ape-like Irish features with contemporary theories of racial development. Less noticed is the rich trawl of images of Irish politicians from the time when Isaac Butt first mounted his Home Rule initiative in the early 1870s, and mustered a surprisingly large party in the 1874 election. Butt, a brilliant Irish lawyer and a far-seeing economist (as well as a part-time novelist) is a quintessential figure in the conquering of London by talented Irish people, even though his was a Pyrrhic victory (see p.43). Success came too late in his life, and political events – not to mention his own party – outpaced him, when he was supplanted by the glamorous and superficially more radical Charles Stewart Parnell. However, Butt represents, yet again, a syndrome well established before the 1870s where bright young Irish politicians came to London, attracted the attention of influential power-brokers (notably Disraeli) and were then often led away from the issues of Irish misgovernment which had provided the material for their electioneering rhetoric in the first place. The novelist Anthony Trollope noted the careers of people like Chichester Fortescue and John Pope-Hennessy, and made the central *arriviste* figure of his political novel-sequence a middle-class Catholic Irishman, Phineas Finn, in the novel of that name (1869). In the 1860s, Finn is a kind of Irish radical who becomes an Irish Whig; though he has made an early stand on the rights

William Butler Yeats, 1865–1939
John Butler Yeats, 1900
Oil on canvas, 770 x
640mm (30³/₈ x 25¹/₄")
National Gallery of Ireland

John Butler Yeats and his
family moved to London in
1867, when William was
two. Apart from Sligo
summers and a brief
return to Dublin in the
early 1880s, the family
eventually settled in the
artistic colony of Bedford
Park, where the artist
continually painted and
drew his talented children.
This is the enduring image
of his eldest son, already
famous as the poet of the
'Celtic Twilight'. J.B. Yeats
(who was renowned for
constantly repainting his
pictures) had evolved an
impressionistic style, which
perfectly conveys the
intense, otherworldly
glamour consciously
projected by the poet.

of Irish tenants, Trollope has him express scepticism about Home Rule in
The Prime Minister (1876). Phineas, the gentlemanly Catholic son of an Irish
doctor, is certainly not an egalitarian, and London has been very good to him
(see p.42). Though Trollope's later embitterment towards Ireland made him
regret creating his Irish hero, he was writing from life; his last, unfinished
novel, *The Landleaguers* (1882), would also revolve around the activities of
Irish members in London, under the new Parnellite dispensation.[10]

The political caricaturists in *Punch* and *Vanity Fair* made much of the Irish
members; but by the 1880s the radicalisation of Home Rule, the advent of
Parnell and, above all, the Land War in Ireland had brought Irish issues more
threateningly into the centre of the London political world. The campaign
begun by Irish tenants in 1879, first to have their rents reduced and then to
gain proprietorial rights over their holdings ('The Land for the People'), struck
an ominous note for the British establishment, and not just for those of them
who owned Irish estates. The Land League's programme was also (erroneously)
connected with the assault on private property apparently threatened by

socialism. Hence the seismic effect when Parnell (who had been president of the Land League as well as leading the Irish Parliamentary Party) achieved his aim of holding the balance of power at Westminster and Gladstone converted to Home Rule (see p.44). In that conversion, the part played by Gladstone's reading of Irish history as relayed by Irish intellectuals such as W.E.H. Lecky (himself, ironically, a Unionist) has been noted; Lecky, indeed, the great historian of eighteenth-century England, also helped to establish Irish history as a subject in its own right (see p.53). But Gladstone was also influenced by, and in turn employed as unofficial publicists, a range of Irish journalists and littérateurs such as T.P. O'Connor, Barry O'Brien and Justin McCarthy – all Irish immigrants closely integrated into London political and social life. McCarthy, a very successful popular historian and novelist as well as a journalist (see p.51), was editor of the *Morning Star* and leader-writer for the *Daily News*, as well as a nationalist MP from 1879 to 1900. O'Connor (see p.47) contributed influential political columns to the *Pall Mall Gazette* and founded the immensely successful *Star*, as well as sustaining a long political career as a Parnellite MP. Ian Sheehy has shown how influential their contacts, and Barry O'Brien's popular historical arguments in pamphlet form, were for Gladstone in his advancement of Home Rule.[11] For their generation, London was a natural magnet. The journalist and war correspondent John Augustus O'Shea, also a Home Ruler, had moved there in 1859 and wrote columns as 'The Irish Bohemian'. He politely contradicted the Dublin nationalist newspaper *United Ireland* in 1892 when it referred to forced emigration: 'When you say [we] had to leave because we were forced to, I must exclude myself ... Even were Ireland as prosperous as I wish it to be, I should have left it. I sailed away because I chose.'[12]

The idea of Irish Home Rule, especially after the apparent threat to property raised by the Land War, could not be stomached by old-style Liberals; Lecky himself was one example and Trollope, by then near the end of his life, reacted violently against it, as his last portrayal of Irish politicians shows. But another kind of presentation of Ireland to London audiences can be tracked through the great treasure trove of Sydney Prior Hall's drawings of the 1888–9 Special Commission hearings into *The Times*'s accusation that Parnell and his party had connived at attempts to assassinate government officials and landlords, as well as crimes against agricultural property, during the Land War.[13] Hall's depiction of what a contemporary journalist described as 'Ireland in the Strand' illustrates the centrality of Irish issues in the political consciousness of the Victorian public. On the one hand, they brought a range of Irish farmers, cottiers, land agents and politicians into the public eye; on the other, they attracted to the courts all sorts of observers, many of them representing the Irish people resident and working in the metropolis. The visitors ranged from Oscar Wilde (see p.45) to Parnell himself, who attended more or less throughout. At exactly the same time (1888), the exhibition halls at Olympia included an 'Irish village', with well-dressed women making elaborate lace in simulacra of Irish cottage interiors (see p.75). 'Virtual' Ireland had established a constant presence in the Victorian metropolis.

Emblematically, John Butler Yeats and his family had returned to London the previous year (1887). The portrait-painter father with his four talented children soon established themselves in the artistic community of Bedford Park, near Hammersmith. The next period, up to Parnell's fall and death in 1891, was to be so vital in W.B. Yeats's artistic formation that he wrote an entire section of his autobiography about it, under the title 'Four Years'. He, like others, used to go to the House of Commons to hear Irish stars like Parnell and the brilliantly vituperative T.M. Healy debate – and when the Parnellite party split in a Westminster committee room over Parnell's citation as co-respondent when his ex-colleague William O'Shea divorced his wife, Katharine, even that fraught occasion was depicted across a double-page spread of the *Illustrated London News*. The scandal shook political life to its foundations; Parnell refused to stand down under pressure from his Liberal allies, the once-great Irish Parliamentary Party split, and their 'Uncrowned King' died suddenly in October 1891, in the midst of violent political infighting, having married Mrs O'Shea a few months before. Yeats's memoir of the 1880s and 1890s can stand, among other things, as a portrait of an era when to be Irish in London was to be at the very centre of things, in terms of political excitement and literary endeavour. But in a sense that was true for the earlier period as well.

Certainly, from the late 1880s a new energy was infused into London's Irish literary and journalistic circles, and Yeats's precocious talent and astonishing energy at 'log-rolling' – boosting his friends' reputations by assiduous reviewing – were key elements. He set himself deliberately to demonstrate that there was a new 'Irish school' of writing, and indefatigably put together collections and anthologies, planted out poems and articles, and wrote endless book reviews for various metropolitan outlets – all to prove this point. But Yeats and his Irish circle in London were, in fact, following in the footsteps of earlier Irish poets and novelists whose popular reputations had reinforced each other, and who had colonised metropolitan literary circles in the decades succeeding the Union. Thomas Moore is of course an emblematic figure, but he had been joined by popular writers like Samuel Lover and Sydney Owenson, who wrote as Lady Morgan (see p.27) and whose novel *The Wild Irish Girl* (1806) created an enduring emblem and trope of Irish glamour and established the outline of historical reconciliation through a 'mixed' marriage, borrowed by many successors.[14] (Owenson herself was firmly pro-Union.) Such writers were stars in their own right by the early years of Victoria's reign, painted and sculpted by the artists of the day. One mid-Victorian Irish writer in London who was a particular inspiration for Yeats was William Allingham (see p.30). His background in Ballyshannon struck a particular chord with a poet who – like all his siblings – thought of Sligo as a lost paradise. Allingham specialised in emigrant verse; he came to England in the 1850s, first settling in Lymington as a customs official, then moving to London. His long narrative poem *Laurence Bloomfield in Ireland* is a sort of novel of ideas in verse about the land question; it appeared in *Fraser's* in 1864 and Allingham became editor of the magazine ten years later, sustaining its Irish identification. Even before then, he was closely involved in the literary and artistic networks around Tennyson and the Pre-Raphaelites (see p.31).

Allingham died just as Yeats too came to London, and Yeats used the publication of collected versions of Allingham's poems to forcefully claim him as an original Irish voice. Allingham's interest in fairy lore was also important to Yeats, principally because of the way Allingham represented Ireland and the supernatural themes in Irish folk culture. Both writers would use this to depict Ireland as exotic, otherworldly and spiritually superior to the materialism of Victorian England. Yeats's first performed play, *The Land of Heart's Desire* (1894), certainly owes something to Allingham as well as to the folk-tales he had been reading, and so does the analysis behind his influential collection of the previous year, *The Celtic Twilight*. Yeats's first famous poem, 'The Lake Isle of Innisfree' (drafted in 1888 and published in 1890), also shows what he learned from Allingham's use of exile-in-London themes, as well as the intricate metres of Samuel Ferguson's and Jeremiah Callanan's translations from the Irish. It is an astonishingly accomplished and original intervention for a poet of twenty-three, but it also follows an established tradition of using Ireland for a London audience. It fits too into a tradition of representing Ireland in a way that deliberately refutes the comic and stage-Irish stereotypes.

This built on well-established foundations as well, notably in drama. The Irish presence on the London stage had been a dominating one since the eighteenth century, in terms of play-writing, acting and theatre management. This continued through the early Victorian period, when actors like Tyrone Power in plays like *The Groves of Blarney* were much celebrated (see pp.28–9). This was followed by the heyday on the London stage of the great Irish actor-manager-playwright Dion Boucicault. The general argument, advanced by Yeats and his colleagues and generally accepted, is that their new-style drama at the very end of the century took on the task of refuting stage-Irish stereotypes:

> We will show that Ireland is not the home of buffoonery and of easy sentiment, as it has been represented, but the home of an ancient idealism, and we are confident of the support of all Irish people, who are weary of misrepresentation, in carrying out a work that is outside all the political questions that divide us.[15]

However, this rather passes over the fact that Boucicault himself was determined to refute these stereotypes too. Certainly, plays like *The Colleen Bawn* (1860), *Arrah-na-Pogue* (1864) and *The Shaughraun* (1874) are melodramatic in construction and far from avant-garde in intention; but, as a Home Ruler and an advocate of amnesty for Fenian prisoners, Boucicault should also be seen as someone committed to presenting his fellow countrymen favourably to London audiences (see p.33). Among the Irish in Britain he was celebrated for doing exactly that, and credited with 'clearing the drama of the "stage Irishman"' and introducing better types of national character to the English stage.[16] Given the huge numbers in his audiences and his hold on popular London theatre, this had a particular importance. *Arrah-na-Pogue*, a particularly interesting play, has a courtroom scene which hinges on different ideas of language held by the Irish and the English, and anticipates actual scenes at the Special Commission some twenty-five years later. Its nationalist content is undisputed, even if the assertion that it was 'banned throughout the British Empire' may be hard to substantiate.[17]

The more obvious impact of Irish dramatists on the London stage, in a genuinely avant-garde manner, comes in the 1890s, when Shaw and Wilde burst on to the scene in their very different ways. Neither used Irish themes (though Shaw would later do so) and both were determined to make English reputations – which they did initially as critics and journalists, and then as creative writers, in the time-honoured Irish pattern. Wilde, however, has recently been re-evaluated as an Irish tale-teller, almost a folklorist (like both his parents); *The Happy Prince* (1888) has been convincingly read in this mode[18] and it appeared just a year after his mother's *Ancient Legends, Mystic Charms and Superstitions of Ireland*. As early as 1891, Yeats resourcefully claimed that Wilde's stories and epigrams proved him the perfect type of 'irresponsible Irishman', and thus connected him to Shaw, two Irishmen who 'keep literary London continually agog to know what they will say next'. (For good measure, Yeats went on to link them both to Whistler, whom he sweepingly claimed as 'half an Irishman also'.)[19]

Wilde owed a good deal to his mother (see p.32), who had been famous in Dublin as a nationalist poet in the mid-century but followed him to London and set up her literary salon in Chelsea, which was frequented by Irish writers including, among others, Katharine Tynan and the young Yeats and his sisters. (They liked the fact that Lady Wilde had two elderly Irish maids who knew everyone's names.) Already, similar people were developing the Irish Literary Society out of the Southwark Irish Literary Club, which had been in existence since 1883. Its founders had in turn built on pre-Yeatsian networks like the circle of Irish writers around *Tinsley's Magazine*, edited in the early 1880s by the Irish publisher Edmund Downey. Francis Fahy was typical of the kind of young Irishman who came to London equipped with success in the Civil Service examinations and an insatiable thirst for metropolitan literary life. Like T.P. O'Connor, he left a memoir delineating this world. Recently edited by Clare Hutton, it vividly conjures up the life of the London Irish in the 1880s: reading all the magazines, sending off their own offerings, frequenting Irish debates at Westminster, persuading Irish MPs to cross the river and speak at their literary society.[20] On one such occasion Justin McCarthy spoke on 'The Literature of 1848' (which meant the Irish Rising of that year, not the European revolutions), chaired by Charles Gavan Duffy, who had been active in the Young Ireland movement a half-century before and was now a retired (and knighted) colonial governor. Oscar Wilde was in the audience, and offered a copy of his mother's *Ancient Legends* to the society's library. Yeats would soon arrive on the scene (introduced by William Morris's son-in-law, whom he knew from Hammersmith's artistic circles); and he would rapidly try to convert the Southwark society to his own purposes, in 1892 forming the Irish Literary

Society, which is still active. But Francis Fahy's and D.J. O'Donoghue's celebratory study of 'Ireland in London', after all, was published (by the Dublin *Evening Telegraph*) in 1889, when Yeats was just starting out.

Some other unlikely Irish influences in London hover around this circle. One is Bram Stoker. He had been a brilliant pupil of John Butler Yeats's great friend the Trinity don Edward Dowden; had married Florence Balcombe, the Dublin beauty courted by Wilde; and had come to London and become Henry Irving's immensely influential manager, the key figure at the Lyceum Theatre and in the high-profile social world that revolved around the Beefsteak Club. Himself a supporter of Home Rule, he was friendly with Justin McCarthy, a stalwart of the Irish Literary Society, close to the whole Wilde family and knew the Yeatses, probably through the Dowden connection; impecunious though they were, the young Yeatses were able to frequent the Lyceum. And Stoker, like so many Irish people in London, was writing stories himself. His first novel, *The Snake's Pass* (1890), was set in the west of Ireland, and was Gladstone's reading matter during the Parnell crisis of 1890–91 (Gladstone, of course, knew Stoker and sent him an enthusiastic letter about it).[21] In 1895 Stoker wrote a gothic horror story which is not about Ireland, but which has been endlessly analysed as a landmark in the Irish gothic tradition; there was a copyright reading of a dramatised version at the Lyceum Theatre on 18 May 1897 (see p.34), though Irving disliked the work and would not back it as a play. (Curiously, Boucicault had already put a vampire on the London stage in 1852, in a play of that name, acted by himself.) No one realised that Stoker would be remembered for *Dracula* when Irving was as good as forgotten; but Stoker's career as yet another Irishman wielding influence in the London artistic world should also be remembered.

George Bernard Shaw may have been more interested in Fabian socialism than in vampire shockers or the Celtic Twilight, but he frequented the same Bedford Park circles as Yeats and knew Stoker through theatre contacts. And his first stunning success, *Arms and the Man*, would be played with Yeats's first performed drama, *The Land of Heart's Desire*, in 1894 – plays featuring Florence Farr, who had love affairs with both the playwrights. This iconic moment is firmly founded in those London-Irish artistic circles, representing a web of contacts that stretches forward to the founding of the Abbey Theatre in Dublin a decade later and back into the world of Bedford Park bohemia. Yeats's play had first been put on, in the Avenue Theatre, as a double bill with another Irish play, *A Comedy of Sighs!* by John Todhunter, also an Irish exile in Bedford Park and a member of the Irish Literary Society. Todhunter, though publicised loyally by Yeats as a 'national writer ... of the Irish race', is now forgotten, and his play was a disaster.[22] But Yeats's little fairy play endures, as does the brilliant image which publicised it, a wonderful poster by Aubrey Beardsley (see p.36), whom Yeats knew through his networks in the Rhymers Club (a group of poets who met in a pub off the Strand) and the *Savoy* magazine. Both were institutions which emphasised the Celtic note and pressed the claims of writers who were Irish, or tried to be (like Lionel Johnson). Moreover, the money behind the production of *Arms and the Man* came from Yeats's friend and fellow occultist the English tea heiress Annie Horniman, who a few years later would bankroll the Abbey Theatre. Yeats's access to high-profile publicity is extraordinary: he managed to get a full page of photographs of the production into the *Sketch* (see p.36). That Beardsley poster image was also used for the next performance, when Todhunter's play was abruptly dropped and *Arms and the Man* was paired with *The Land of Heart's Desire*. The lovely Bernard Partridge watercolour of Shaw watching the rehearsals, with a great smile on his face, shows a man who knows he has arrived (see p.13). The same year, 1894, saw a run of Wilde's plays get under way, culminating with *The Importance of Being Earnest* in early 1895. This, of course, coincided with his terrible trial, disgrace and imprisonment; suddenly, towards the end of the run, the author's name stopped appearing on the elaborate theatre programme.

Yeats and Shaw, by contrast, were just at the outset of their dazzling careers as Irish writers in London. Yeats had established his circle of Irish authors, had colonised and dominated the Irish Literary Society, had published anthologies of the new Irish poets and had started to work up a network of publishing contacts. He was famous, and his Celtic and mystical image was preserved in quintessential 1890s images like the drawing of him as a mage by Althea Gyles (see p.37), yet another Irish artist who had come to London to make her fortune. His father was painting portraits, which would culminate in the abiding image of his brilliant elder son in 1900 (see p.17); his sisters were learning the arts which would enable them to set up the Dun Emer Industries and the Cuala Press back in Dublin, where the principles absorbed in William Morris's Hammersmith workshop would be put to Irish uses – printing, embroidering and illustrating in a distinctly Irish manner. His brother, Jack Yeats, not long out of his teens, was making precocious illustrations for the London comic papers (see p.34). W.B. Yeats would always henceforth publish the first, limited edition of his works with his sisters' press. But equally consistently, he would maintain his major publishers in London, and spend a large part of each year there. It was where, after all, his reputation had been made.

Around 1900, according to the novelist George Moore, the sceptre of intelligence returned from London to Dublin (see p.37). Moore himself was another brilliant Irishman who had made a great splash in London literary circles: an early novel, *A Drama in Muslin* (1886), had actually used the Irish Land War as a subject, though the realist novels which made his reputation, such as *A Mummer's Wife* (1885) and *Esther Waters* (1894), followed French models and were set in England. Moore was also a great advocate of the new French painting, and in that he was echoed by the Irish connoisseur Hugh Lane, who from the early 1900s was determined to bring modern art to Dublin – as his aunt Augusta Gregory, co-founder with Yeats of the Irish Literary Theatre and the Abbey, was determined to bring a dramatic revelation. We stand on the edge of a new era here: the point at which, according to Yeats's later memory, everyone came down off their 1890s stilts. Victoria was dead, and the Irish were carrying the torch back to Dublin. Two symbolic events, as a kind of epilogue, might be the art exhibition masterminded by Hugh Lane at Guildhall in 1904, bringing Irish painters to

London, and the wildly successful visit to the capital of the Irish National Theatre Society (just about to be reconstituted as the Abbey Theatre), presenting radically economical new plays by Yeats and John Millington Synge. The style of acting, and the very appearance of the strikingly spare and tasteful playbill and programme, symbolised a rejection of old-style theatrical modes, inescapably if not always fairly associated with their predecessor Boucicault. As Max Beerbohm wrote:

> With perfect simplicity, perfect dignity and composure, they were just themselves. Just themselves; and how could such Irish selves not be irresistible? Several of our metropolitan players are Irish, and even they, however thickly coated with Saxonism, have a charm for us beyond their Saxon-blooded fellows. The Irish people, unspoiled, in their own island – who can resist them? But footlights heighten every effect; and behind them unspoiled Irish people win us quicklier and more absolutely than ever. And behind London footlights! There they have not merely their own charm, but that charm also which belongs to all exotics.[23]

The Irish presence was now not only avant-garde but 'exotic'. Attitudes had shifted radically on both sides of the Irish Sea. Dublin was in a state of cultural assertiveness and activity which makes Joyce's famous description of it as a 'centre of paralysis' look very partial indeed. In the early 1890s, Yeats and others had been embroiled in a controversy which occupied many newspaper column inches under the title 'The Irish Intellectual Capital – Where is It?'[24] At that point, the case for London's claims could still be made (albeit mischievously). After the turn of the century, it was clear that Dublin had become the focus for Irish cultural energy.

This was the point when Irish nationalist writers like W.P. Ryan and D.P. Moran, though themselves part of the recent emigration to Britain, began to condemn the Home Rule generation of O'Connor, McCarthy and O'Brien as deracinated collaborators, corrupted by British materialism.[25] Ryan had once been employed by O'Connor in London, but lampooned him in his satirical novel *The Plough and the Cross* (1910), kissing his hand to Erin from his editorial office in London.[26] Moran, also from a London-Irish background but also returned to Ireland, attacked him in similar terms in his new journal advocating an Irish-Ireland, the *Leader*. The new Celtic aesthetic, with modernist overtones and a deliberate repudiation of Victorian values, was taking over, and it could carry radical nationalist messages too. Nonetheless, many of its most prominent advocates had spent their youth or learned their trade in London.

Yeats himself, moving in to his set of rooms near Euston Station in 1896 (see p.38), informed friends that he would stay there for at most two years and then go back to Ireland. But he stayed in Woburn Buildings for twenty-two years, and did not return to Ireland until 1922. And when he was looking for a new play to open the Abbey in 1904, he turned first to his old London-Irish ally and rival Shaw. Shaw mischievously produced *John Bull's Other Island* – far too sarcastic, sceptical and politically abrasive to broadcast the right message. Significantly, the Irish protagonist, Larry Doyle, is an engineer who has made a good life in London and has 'an instinct against going back to Ireland ... I'd rather go to the South Pole than Rosscullen.' The play was diplomatically steered back to London itself, where it had a surprising success in that same *annus mirabilis* of 1904 (see p.39). The Prime Minister, Arthur Balfour (who had been a notoriously efficient Chief Secretary for Ireland and knew the country well), came five times. At a royal command performance for King Edward the following year, the monarch laughed so hard he broke a chair. It is unlikely that he realised how much fun Shaw was having at the expense of England, as well as ridiculing everything Irish, from the Irish Parliamentary Party to the Catholic Church to the Gaelic League. London was allowing the playwright the traditional licence extended to Irish entertainers and commentators at work in the Victorian metropolis, and he was making the most of it. *John Bull's Other Island* is also a violently modern work, expressing the contradictions, exploitations and dependencies of the Union like nothing else. But at the same time it comes out of a world of opportunity, influence and privilege which London opened to a certain kind of Irish person, and which deserves to be fully recognised.

NOTES

1 Curtis (1997); Gilley (1978); Hickman (1999); O'Day (1993).
2 McCormack (1980); Gray (2004).
3 Shaw (2001), p.11.
4 O'Day (1990), p.11.
5 His name was Michael MacDonagh: O'Donnell (1910), Vol.I, pp.174–6.
6 Edwards and Storey (1985).
7 Ebrington (1783–1861), later 2nd Earl Fortescue, and Duncannon (1809–80), later 5th Earl of Bessborough, were both Whig MPs at this time, allied to O'Connellites.
8 Curtis (2003), pp.88–9.
9 Butler (1922), p.199.
10 Foster (1993), pp.143–52, 292–6; Foster (2001), pp.127–47.
11 Sheehy (2003), *passim*; Sheehy (2004).
12 *United Ireland*, 8 April 1892, quoted Sheehy (2003), p.22.
13 Cullen (2004), pp.189–98, 209–13.
14 See Owenson (2000) for Connolly and Copley's important Introduction.
15 Original manifesto of Irish Literary Theatre, drafted by Yeats, quoted in full in Foster (1997), p.184.
16 O'Sullivan (1993), Vol.III, p.18.
17 Deane (1991), Vol.II, p.234.
18 Toomey (1998).
19 Frayne, Vol.I (1970), p.205.
20 Hutton (2002); also Foster (1997), pp.79ff.
21 Belford (1996), p.230.
22 Kelly and Domville (1986), pp.122–3.
23 Quoted in full in Foster (1997), pp.318–19.
24 Frayne, Vol.I (1970), pp.122–5.
25 Foster (1993), pp.296–3; Sheehy (2003), Ch.1.
26 Sheehy (2004), p.76.

Literature and journalism

faithfully yours,
William Maginn
16. 4. 1830
Sketched Delroy

William Maginn, 1793–1842
Daniel Maclise, 1830
Pencil and watercolour, 274 x 187mm (10³/₄ x 7³/₈")
National Portrait Gallery, London (NPG 5513)

In 1830 in London, Maginn helped found the high Tory literary journal *Fraser's Magazine*.
He was one of a number of Irish contributors, but is mainly associated with its highly
popular 'Gallery of Illustrious Literary Characters', many of whom were illustrated by
Maclise (under the pseudonym of Alfred Croquis). This drawing appeared as no.8 in the
series and ended with the following comment: *'Floreat Doctor!* – Long may he continue at
once the star of our erudition, our philosophy, and our dialectics, and, in his own
immortal words, – "A randy, bandy, brandy, no Dandy, Rollicking jig of an Irishman!"'

Sydney Owenson, Lady Morgan, c.1778–1859
Pierre-Jean David d'Angers, 1829–30
Marble, height 610mm (24")
Victoria & Albert Museum

The Fraserians
Daniel Maclise, 1835
Pencil on paper, 215 x 280mm (8¹/₂ x 11")
Victoria & Albert Museum

Maclise's drawing is a wonderful pulling together of many of the Irish writers, journalists and hacks who contributed to one of London's leading journals of the pre-Victorian period, *Fraser's Magazine*. The entrepreneurial careers of such Irishmen as William Maginn, who stands at the back, Francis Sylvester Mahony (aka Father Prout), Thomas Crofton Croker and Maclise himself are suggested in this round table of writers and satirists, some of whom are William Harrison Ainsworth, Thomas Carlyle, J.G. Lockhart, Robert Southey, William Makepeace Thackeray and Samuel Taylor Coleridge. The drawing appeared in *Fraser's* 'Gallery of Illustrious Literary Characters', January 1835 – a series which included other Irish literary stars, such as Lady Morgan and Caroline Norton.

This spirited bust of Ireland's most successful early nineteenth-century novelist by a leading French sculptor of the period suggests the international fashion for the romantic Ireland that Morgan created. In *The Wild Irish Girl: A National Tale*, first published in London in 1806, Owenson combined an interest in antiquarianism with a condemnation of English stereotypes of Ireland. In an 1846 London reissue of that celebrated book, the author claimed that this was the 'first attempt at a genuine Irish novel', which then created a literary tradition 'founded on national grievances and borne out by historical fact'. Visiting Paris in 1829, Owenson commissioned this bust from David, who also produced a bronze medallion and a plaster version of the marble, both of which are in the Galerie David d'Angers in Angers.

Tyrone Power as Connor O'Gorman in *The Groves of Blarney*
Nicholas Crowley, 1838
Oil on canvas, 635 x 762mm (25 x 30")
Tyrone Guthrie Centre at Annaghmakerrig

This painting is a particularly striking example of the glamorous (and exotic) representation of the Irish presence on the Victorian stage – a great Irish actor (Tyrone Power, 1797–1841) in a fashionable Irish play presenting Ireland at its most romantic. Anna Maria Hall's farce focuses on the charming hero, O'Gorman, played by Power, who is seated on the right dressed in a velvet coat with gold frogging, lace cuffs and a scarlet waistcoat. Crowley moved from Dublin to London in 1837 and exhibited this portrait group at the British Institution in 1840.

THEATRE ROYAL ADELPHI

Proprietors, Messrs. YATES & GLADSTANE.　Under the Management of Mr. YATES.

Mr. YATES is happy to announce the return (to his Engagement) of

Mr. POWER

who will continue his performances at this Theatre till its close, and will make his First Appearance This Evening, in

A NEW IRISH DRAMA in Three Acts!

FIRST APPEARANCES of Mr. DENVIL & Mrs. HOOPER.

☞ First Night of THE BOY AND THE BANDITS!

On EASTER-MONDAY, April 16, 1838. and during the Week,

Will be produced (for the FIRST TIME) a Serio Comic Romantic Burletta, in Three Acts, written by Mrs. S. C. HALL, and founded on the leading story in her "*Lights and Shadows of Irish Life,*" entitled The

GROVES OF BLARNEY

TIME—TWO DAYS—1740,　Scene, ...THE VILLAGE OF BLARNEY.

The OVERTURE composed by WILLIAM FORDE.　The VOCAL MUSIC by ALEXANDER D. ROCHE.
The SCENERY by Mr. PITT and Assistants, from Sketches by T. CROFTON CROKER, Esq.

THE PIECE PRODUCED UNDER THE IMMEDIATE DIRECTION OF Mr. YATES.

Connor O'Gorman, ... (a true hearted Irishman) .... Mr. POWER,
Marcus Roche, ... (his Friend) .. Mr. O. SMITH,
Ulick O'Sullivan, ... (his Rival, the last of his race) .... Mr. DENVIL, from the Theatre Royal, Covent Garden,
Peter Swan, (a Cockney Traveller, in search of the Picturesque, among the WILD IRISH) Mr. WILKINSON,
Mick Sweeny, (a collector of rent) Mr. SANDERS,　Dennis Murphy, (one of the real pipers) Mr. CULLENFORD,
Tom Staff, (a Boy in the service of the Factor) Mr. UDELL,　Jack Gale, ("coadjutor" of the same) Mr. GEORGE,
Terry Conroy, (a follower of the same) Mr. WILLIAMS,　Hector Lee, (the Son of Margaret) Master JOHNSON,
Capt. Grey, (an English Officer) Mr. LANSDOWNE,　Capt. Rowland, (recruiting for Foreign Service) Mr. CATHIE.
Margaret Lee, (a Young English Widow residing at Blarney, and beloved by Connor O'Gorman) Mrs. HOOPER,
(From the Theatre Royal, Drury Lane,)
Flora Russel, (her Sister, with the Song of "When Lovers come to woo a Maid") Miss SHAW,
Aileen O'Sullivan, .. { (the Sister of Ulick, with the Songs of "Aileen Mavourneen" } .. Miss A. TAYLOR,
and "A Blessing and a Tear,")
The Griffin, ... (Mother of Mischief) .... Mr. YATES,
Old Monica, ... Miss WARREN,　Soldiers, Constables, Peasant Girls, &c.

Act 1.---BLARNEY BRIDGE!

"WHERE NO WATER FLOWS."

BLARNEY CASTLE IN THE DISTANCE.

A ready made "Tower" in Ireland—Song, Miss SHAW, "When Lovers come to woo a Girl."

THE BEE'S NEST.

COTTAGE OF MARGARET LEE!

Blarney Stone—The great Irish smoothing Iron—Tricks upon Travellers—Song, Mr. POWER, "The Perilous Blarney"—The Ogre with a Man to it.

VAULTS OF BLARNEY CASTLE

Song.—Miss A. TAYLOR, "Aileen Mavourneen."—Connor tempted to take a drop—The Spirits that work evil—An Irishman's blunders — of the head and not the heart.

THE CROMECK OF THE GIANT'S BED.

A bit of a "Shindy"—Irish arguments—The Factor paid, and gets something for himself.

Act 2.---"The Sweet Rock-Close!"

AND WITCHES' STAIRS!

Song.—Miss A. TAYLOR, "A blessing and a tear."—Witches—dead and living—Mischief, and the mother of Mischief, on foot.

THE CHAMBER OF MARGARET LEE.

The Stolen Treasure!

Cabin of Monica Murphy - - Over-running the Constable—A Traveller's troubles.

The Groves of Blarney, 1838
Playbill, 338 x 206mm (13¹/₄ x 8¹/₈")
Theatre Museum (Victoria & Albert Museum)

The Groves of Blarney by Anna Maria Hall (1800–81) was first performed at the Adelphi
Theatre, London, on 16 April 1838. The play is loosely based on a story of the same name
in her book of Irish stories, *Lights and Shadows of Irish Life* (1838). The farce deals with
disguise, a kidnapping, a secret society and a sensational rescue.

William Allingham, 1824–89
Helen Allingham, 1876
Watercolour, 292 x 235mm (11½ x 9¼")
National Portrait Gallery, London (NPG 1647)

William Allingham was a Donegal-born poet who spent much of his life as a customs official in Ireland. He moved to London in 1870 and became editor of *Fraser's Magazine*. Earlier he had been closely involved with the Pre-Raphaelite group and a great friend of Thomas Carlyle. In 1874 he married Helen Paterson, an illustrator and watercolourist. Allingham's most ambitious work is his long fictional poem *Laurence Bloomfield in Ireland* (1864), which carries vivid descriptions of rural Irish evictions and first appeared serially in *Fraser's Magazine*. Its publication led to his being awarded a Civil List pension. Helen Allingham is well known for her depictions of English country cottages and gardens.

The Harp That Once through Tara's Halls

F.P. Becker after Daniel Maclise, 1846
Engraving for Thomas Moore's *Irish Melodies* (Longman, Brown, Green, and Longman's, London, 14th edn., p.13); height 275mm (10⅞")
The British Library

Maclise's illustrations for a new edition of the *Irish Melodies* are the quintessential demonstration of the shaping of Irish fashionability to English purposes. This page shows a feudal yet civilised Ireland populated by a king, a harpist and beautiful maidens.

The Fairies, a Nursery Song

Dalziel brothers, after Arthur Hughes, 1855
Wood-engraved illustration to William Allingham's poem in his book *The Music Master, A Love Story, and Two Series of Day and Night Songs* (Routledge, London, 1855, p.20); height 166mm (6½")
The British Museum, London

Hughes's illustration of dancing elves is a small yet exquisite example of the popularity of Allingham's verse at the high point of Pre-Raphaelite activity. The image illustrates his famous fairy poem:

> Up the Airy Mountain
> Down the rushy glen,
> We daren't go a-hunting
> For fear of little men.

An Irish setting is made clear by the references to sights around Donegal Bay, while the poem is illustrated by a leading English artist for an important London publisher. Containing other illustrations by Dante Gabriel Rossetti and John Everett Millais, this publication has been referred to as a 'landmark' in Victorian illustration.

Jane Francesca Elgee, Lady Wilde (Speranza), 1821–96
George Morosini, c.1880
Crayon on paper, 190 x 124mm (7$\frac{1}{2}$ x 4$\frac{7}{8}$")
National Gallery of Ireland

This drawing is one of the best-known representations of Lady Wilde, who, after the death of her husband in 1879, followed her son, Oscar, to London and held soirées in her London home. Shaw and Yeats attended these gatherings and she contributed poems and articles to *The Woman's World*, of which her son was editor (1887–9). Morosini was an Italian artist who settled in Dublin and exhibited at the Royal Hibernian Academy.

No 11

MR DION BOUCICAULT
(IN THE SHAUGHRAUN)

Washon & Macdonald, Printed Publishers London

Dion Boucicault as Conn the Shaughraun
Alfred Bryan, c.1875
Autolithograph, 350 x 235mm (13³/₄ x 9¹/₄")
National Portrait Gallery, London

Dionysius Lardner Boucicault (1820–90) wrote more than 140 plays that were produced
in London, Dublin and New York. He was a master of the so-called 'sensational drama' so
beloved of Victorian theatregoers, yet at the same time he was determined to elevate the
'stage-Irish' characterisation of his fellow countrymen in British drama. His three great
'Irish' plays are *The Colleen Bawn* (1860), *Arrah-na-Pogue* (1864) and *The Shaughraun* (1874).
He is seen here as Conn, the hero of *The Shaughraun* (meaning a 'vagabond'), which he
played in London in 1875 at the Drury Lane Theatre. Alfred Bryan was a major
contributor to such journals as the *Illustrated Sporting and Dramatic News* (founded in
1874), where he would illustrate the drama reviews with humorous portraits.

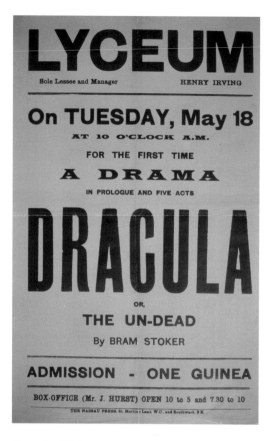

Dracula, 1897
Poster, 505 x 320mm (19⁷/₈ x 12⁵/₈")
Royal Shakespeare Company

This poster for the first public reading of Bram Stoker's
Dracula, in 1897, confirms the entrepreneurial presence of
Irish writers in London in the late nineteenth century. The
play-reading at Henry Irving's Lyceum Theatre was a one-
off occasion so that Stoker (1847–1912) could maintain
control of a text that was to become iconic.

An East End Theatre: Saturday Night
Jack B. Yeats, 1891
Wood engraving in *Ariel, or The London Puck*, 11 July 1891,
p.27; height 304mm (12")
The British Library

This page-sized humorous illustration for a London
popular journal shows exactly the kind of work by which
the young Yeatses supported themselves in the late-
Victorian London marketplace. It also suggests many of
the characteristics of Yeats's later draughtsmanship, which
include a delight in filling the whole composition and a
striking use of light and shade, as well as a taste for
observing the pastimes of 'lowlife'. For at least a year
between January 1890 and February 1892, Yeats worked
for Israel Zangwill, the editor of *Ariel*, and contributed
about six illustrations on the theme of 'Round the Town'.

Oscar Wilde, 1854–1900
W. & D. Downey, published 1891
Carbon print, 139 x 93mm (5¹/₂ x 3⁵/₈")
National Portrait Gallery, London (NPG x27397)

Based in Newcastle upon Tyne, the Downey brothers attracted the patronage of
the royal family and moved to London in 1881, where they set up a studio in
Ebury Street, near Buckingham Palace. Published at the commencement of Wilde's
period of high fame, when he was thirty-seven, this photograph appeared in the
same year as his only novel, *The Picture of Dorian Gray*, his essays *Intentions*, *The Soul
of Man under Socialism* and *Lord Arthur Savile's Crime, and Other Stories*. He was now
firmly established as a self-styled 'Professor of Aesthetics', on a mocking mission to
civilise the barbarian English upper classes. In this *annus mirabilis*, he also wrote
Lady Windermere's Fan, and his great success as a playwright was just about to
begin. But 1891 was also the year when he met his nemesis, Lord Alfred Douglas.

A Comedy of Sighs! and The Land of Heart's Desire
Aubrey Beardsley, 1894
Poster, 775 x 520mm (30¹/₂ x 20¹/₂")
Victoria & Albert Museum

This poster for the Avenue Theatre production of
Todhunter's *A Comedy of Sighs!* and Yeats's *The Land of
Heart's Desire* brings together (in a West End venue) an
Irish writer of the older Victorian school (Todhunter was
a member of the Yeats circle in Bedford Park), the first
performed play of the young W.B.Yeats and the design
genius of Yeats's friend Aubrey Beardsley, crystallising a
moment in 1890s culture when Irish writers were just on
the edge of colonising contemporary drama. *The Land of
Heart's Desire* would be put on a few weeks later with the
premiere of Shaw's dazzling *Arms and the Man*, and Wilde's
An Ideal Husband and *The Importance of Being Earnest*
appeared within a few months. Yeats retained Beardsley's
mysterious image for the cover of Fisher Unwin's
published version of the play that year. The poster/playbill
is a powerful emblem of the arrival of Irish dramatic
talent at the centre of London drama in the 1890s.

The Land of Heart's Desire
Photographs by Hills and Saunders, London, from the
Sketch, 25 April 1894, 349 x 255mm (13³/₄ x 10")
Theatre Museum (Victoria & Albert Museum)

Yeats's 'faery' play, written the year after his landmark
The Celtic Twilight was published, used themes of supernatural child-stealing, otherworldliness and anti-materialism
to represent on the London stage an exotic Ireland
of legends and dreams. But it was publicised as
hard-headedly as all his works, using an impressive
range of metropolitan contacts.

W. B. Yeats, 1865–1939
Althea Gyles, 1899
Pen, ink and wash on board, 245 x 166mm (9⁵/₈ x 6¹/₂")
The British Museum, London

Trained at the Slade, Gyles was an Irish contemporary of
Yeats's in bohemian circles in 1890s London. She designed
the art-nouveau binding of Yeats's breakthrough collection,
The Wind Among the Reeds, in 1899. This drawing, from the
same year, portrays her friend as a mage, with a mystic
rose. Originally intended for the frontispiece, it is an
unusual and striking image of one 1890s London Irish
artist by another, consciously fashioned to emphasise his
otherworldly glamour and sexual allure. Gyles was a
convinced occultist, with an erratic and self-destructive
private life. She worked closely with Yeats on the
iconography of his early book covers, and he believed that
she completely understood his symbolism.

Mr W.B. Yeats Presenting Mr George Moore
to the Queen of the Fairies
Max Beerbohm, c.1904
Pen and watercolour on paper, 318 x 197mm (12¹/₂ x 7³/₄")
Dublin City Gallery, The Hugh Lane

This famous cartoon brings together two London-based
leading figures of the Irish cultural renaissance, W.B. Yeats
and George Moore (1852–1933), as seen by a brilliant
cultural commentator (who also publicised the first Abbey
Players' tour in England). As a central image in the
marketing of Irish fashionability in London at the turn of
the century, it was judged by the *Athenaeum* 'exquisite in
its observation'.

YOUNG IRELAND IN LONDON
Mr. W. B. Yeats in his Study in Woburn Buildings.

Young Ireland in London: Mr W.B. Yeats in his Study in Woburn Buildings
Photograph in the *Tatler*, 12: 157, 29 June 1904, p.523; height 368mm (14¹/₂")
The British Library

This photograph of W.B. Yeats is a key image of the poet in the centre of his London operations, surrounded by carefully assembled iconic images, including Dante's death mask, Blake engravings and one of the huge white paschal candles that illuminated his weekly salon on Monday evenings.

George Bernard Shaw, 1856–1950
Alvin Langdon Coburn, 1904
Photogravure, 202 × 158mm (7³/₄ × 6¹/₄")
The Royal Photographic Society Collection at the National Museum of Photography, Film & Television

This photograph is celebratory and reflective. It captures Shaw in intense mood, head and shoulders, staring at the camera. In 1904, he had a great success with *John Bull's Other Island*, his one full-length play about Ireland. He was beginning to conquer (to use his own phrase) the London stage. The taking of this portrait in August 1904 is described by Shaw in his letters and he went so far as to suggest that Coburn was 'the best photographer in the world'. This portrait later appeared in Coburn's celebrated collection *Men of Mark* (1913), along with a portrait of that other successful Irishman, W.B. Yeats.

Politics

A Family Group
John Doyle, 1835
Lithograph, 427 x 290mm (16³/₄ x 11³/₈")
National Portrait Gallery, London

This print of Daniel O'Connell with two prominent Irish Whig politicians, Lords
Ebrington and Duncannon, is subtitled 'Framed, glazed and ready to be hung up at
Brooke's [sic] Club', and shows how O'Connell's compact with the reforming Whig
government brought him into the centre of political power-broking – and only six years
after his exertions had won Catholics like himself the right to sit in Parliament. It was
published in London on 10 June 1835. Born in Dublin, the London-based cartoonist John
Doyle was known to his contemporaries as HB (a monogram created by placing two 'JD's
one above the other, 'J' being a conventional initial for John).

Daniel O'Connell, 1775–1847
Sir George Hayter, 1834
Oil on millboard, 356 x 305mm (14 x 12")
National Portrait Gallery, London (NPG 4582)

O'Connell's iconography is extensive, with numerous images produced from as early as
1800 until well after his death. This profiled pose of the head of the 'Liberator' is a study
for his appearance in the front row of the opposition benches of Hayter's huge canvas in
the National Portrait Gallery (NPG 54), which represents the meeting of the newly
reformed Parliament that took place in February 1833. Images of O'Connell were not
hard to find in London: caricatured portrayals were rampant; a David Wilkie portrait was
shown at the RA in 1838, Hayter's painting was exhibited in 1843 and entered the
National Portrait Gallery in 1858, while J.P. Haverty's full-length work was given to the
Reform Club, possibly in the 1850s, by John O'Connell, Daniel's third son.

" But you Irish fellows always ride."

Phineas Finn. Chap. xxiv. Page 119.

'But you Irish fellows always ride'
John Everett Millais, 1868
Wood engraving for *Phineas Finn* in *Saint Paul's Magazine*,
2, 1868, opp. p.119; height 225mm (8⁷/₈")
The British Library

This illustration to Anthony Trollope's novel *Phineas Finn*
shows the Irish MP sitting on the bed of Lord Chiltern,
who has been injured while riding. Trollope's presentation
of an Irish hero in his bestselling 'Palliser' political novels
counteracts many of the supposed stereotypes of the
Irish in England, and Millais's romantic illustrations carry
through the point. Phineas, a middle-class Irish Catholic,
moves easily through high political society; though
his moral sense is sometimes slightly off-beam, his career
is made through charm, physical attractiveness and a
basic honesty.

Isaac Butt, 1813–79
John Butler Yeats, 1876
Chalk, 425 x 349mm (16³/₄ x 13³/₄")
National Portrait Gallery, London (NPG 3831)

The founder of the Irish Home Rule movement, Butt was leader of the Irish
Parliamentary Party at Westminster in the generation before the excitement of the
Parnell era. His idea of Home Rule began as a federalist initiative, keeping Ireland securely
within the empire while having her own parliament and a large degree of autonomy. As a
struggling artist, Yeats was hoping that a portrait of such a prestigious sitter would lead
to greater things. This was not to be, and at the time Butt himself was facing the
challenge of more impatient Irish MPs, who would radicalise both the party and the
nature of the Home Rule demand.

HIBERNIA CONSOLATRIX.

Hibernia Consolatrix

John Tenniel, 1886

Wood engraving in *Punch*, 90, 5 June 1886, p.271; height 283mm (11 1/8")

National Portrait Gallery, London

Ireland in the guise of a barefoot milkmaid consoles the weary and unhorsed knight, William Gladstone, whose Home Rule Bill for Ireland would be finally defeated three days later.

Oscar Wilde, 1854–1900
Sydney Prior Hall, 1889
Pencil on paper, 172 x 204mm (6³/₄ x 8")
National Portrait Gallery, London (NPG 2265)

Hall's drawing of the Irish poet and playwright was made while Wilde attended the
hearings of the year-long Parnell Commission in Probate Court Number 1 at the Royal
Courts of Justice on London's Strand. The Commission was set up to investigate alleged
connections between Charles Stewart Parnell, leader of the Irish Parliamentary Party at
Westminster, and crime. The allegations were eventually dropped and Parnell was cleared.
Sydney Prior Hall, one of the leading illustrators of the period, was commissioned by the
Graphic, an illustrated London journal, to supply images for the year-long proceedings.
A surprising cross-section of elite society attended the hearings at the Strand, including
several other Irish celebrities. Hall's drawing of Wilde appeared in the *Graphic* on
16 February 1889, in the centre of a long column describing the testimony of a government
spy. Wilde himself does not feature in the text; he is but an element of a larger design.

The Great Powers Combine against England
Sydney Prior Hall, 1887
Pencil and gouache on paper, 304 x 319mm (12 x 12⅝")
National Gallery of Ireland

This drawing and that on p.55 reflect the powerful Irish presence in the House of
Commons in the 1880s. Hall shows a group of Irish MPs, sitting in the opposition
benches, discussing tactics during the debate on the Irish Criminal Law and Procedure
Bill, April 1887. The ironic title humorously belittles the impact that the Irish
Parliamentary Party of over eighty MPs actually had at the time (in the previous
parliament, they had held the balance, forcing Gladstone to adopt Home Rule). From left
to right we see John Redmond, John Dillon, John G. Swift MacNeill, T.P. O'Connor and
Timothy Healy (who would be suspended from the House on 15 April).

Thomas Power O'Connor, 1848–1929
Sir Leslie Ward ('Spy'), 1888
Watercolour, 305 × 181mm (12 × 7¹/₈")
National Portrait Gallery, London (NPG 3127)

This watercolour drawing by Spy, one of the leading caricaturists for *Vanity Fair*, first appeared on 25 February 1888. O'Connor was a journalist and nationalist MP who combined radical and Home Rule politics, as well as founding and editing mass-circulation papers like the *Star*, *T.P.'s Weekly* and *M.A.P.* (Mainly About People), which featured unadulterated gossip. A Liverpool MP for many years, he eventually became Father of the House of Commons.

Charles Stewart Parnell, 1846–91
Sydney Prior Hall, 1892
Oil on canvas, 1120 x 860mm (44 x 33⁷/₈")
National Gallery of Ireland

This three-quarter-length oil portrait of Parnell is the impressive result of Hall's many years of studying him in the imperial parliament as well as at the Parnell Commission of 1888–9. In fact, in this portrait the head is possibly derived from one of Hall's drawings taken on the spot at the Royal Courts of Justice, now in the National Portrait Gallery (NPG 2229). However, given the date and the fact that Parnell is crumpling a sheet of parliamentary order papers which prominently displays the royal crest, this posthumous portrait represents the Irish leader's break with Gladstone and apparent repudiation of parliamentary tactics during his last campaign of 1890–91.

The Parnell Commission: Charles Stewart Parnell (1846–91), Sir George Henry Lewis, 1st Baronet (1833–1911) and Thomas Miller Beach (Major le Caron) (1841–94)
Sydney Prior Hall, 1889
Pencil on paper, 292 x 457mm (11½ x 18")
National Portrait Gallery, London (NPG 2244)

This is one of Hall's most memorable drawings of the Parnell Commission and was reproduced in the *Graphic* on 16 February 1889. Parnell, who was by now known for a certain eccentric carelessness in his dress, is wearing his old coat and is accompanied by his solicitor, Sir George Lewis. Approaching the entrance to the Royal Courts of Justice on the Strand (with its business-as-usual notice 'Chambers to Let') and absorbed in discussion, they ignore the government spy 'Major Le Caron', standing off to the right, whose evidence was one of the high points of the Commission's hearings.

Imitation the Sincerest Flattery
(Effects of a Long Session in the House)
Harry Furniss, 1890
Pen and ink on paper, 275 × 225mm (10^7/$_8$ × 8^7/$_8$")
Victoria & Albert Museum

Born in Wexford, Furniss made his name as a contributor to *Punch*, where this caricature appeared on 23 August 1890. It focuses on body movement as a definition of political allegiance and shows three sides of the House of Commons in 1890: top row: the Liberals (then in opposition), who all copy W.E. Gladstone as in the 'effect of Gladstonianism'; middle row: the Tory front bench, who ape Arthur Balfour, then Chief Secretary for Ireland; bottom row: the Irish members, who have taken on 'Healyism', a histrionic debating style much enjoyed by Irish observers who attended debates – including the young W.B. Yeats. From left to right we see Timothy Healy, John Dillon, Dr C.K.D. Tanner, John Redmond, John O'Connor and Thomas Sexton.

Justin McCarthy, 1830–1912
Walery (Stanislas Julian Walery, Count Ostrorog), 1890
Carbon print, 247 x 179mm (9³/₄ x 7")
National Portrait Gallery, London (NPG x9418)

This portrait of Justin McCarthy appeared in London in April 1890 in a monthly series, *Our Celebrities*. Walery was renowned for the precision of his photographs, which were usually taken in his studio at 164 Regent Street. McCarthy followed an influential career as a journalist in London with an equally prominent political life: a nationalist MP from 1879 to 1900, he briefly led the Irish Parliamentary Party after Parnell's fall. Throughout he followed a parallel track as a popular novelist and historian; several of his novels were clearly intended to educate British opinion about Ireland, and his five-volume *History of Our Own Times* (1879) was an enduring bestseller.

Edward Henry Carson, 1854–1935
Sir Robert Ponsonby Staples, Bt, 1898
Chalk, 311 x 413mm (12¼ x 16¼")
National Portrait Gallery, London (NPG 5476)

The Dublin-educated lawyer Edward Carson and the Cookstown, County Tyrone-born
aristocrat-cum-artist Ponsonby Staples were friends in London and this splendid chalk
drawing was made over two sittings in the artist's studio at Rutland Gate in
Knightsbridge. At the time, Carson was Unionist MP for Dublin University and had
recently led the case against his fellow Dubliner Oscar Wilde in the famous trial of 1895.
Carson was later celebrated as the leader of Ulster Unionism.

William Edward Hartpole Lecky, 1838–1903
John Lavery, 1903
Oil on canvas, 630 x 480mm (24³/₄ x 18⁷/₈")
National Gallery of Ireland

Lecky was one of the great Irish intellectuals of the age. He came to fame as the slightly
sardonic chronicler of the 'rise of rationalism' and wrote a strikingly broad-minded
History of European Morals (1869). But above all his history of the eighteenth century and
other writings about Ireland had a profound effect on Gladstone and indeed the whole
Home Rule generation. Yet Lecky himself, a fixture in the London establishment (and a
trustee of the National Portrait Gallery), was a convinced Unionist; he came from an Irish
landowning family and was eventually disillusioned with the political Liberalism which he
did much to define. Here he is painted by another Irishman, Lavery, who exhibited the
portrait (a year after the sitter's death) at the important 1904 London Guildhall
exhibition of Irish artists.

From mythical abstractions
to modern realities:
depicting the Irish émigrée
Fintan Cullen

One of the more dramatic images produced by Sydney Prior Hall during his many years as an illustrator of London public events is a pencil and gouache drawing of the Irish radical MP John Dillon being ordered to leave the House of Commons on 3 February 1881 (see opposite). Dillon's biographer, F.S.L. Lyons, has referred to him as the 'intrepid spokesman of the agrarian left'[1] and his suspension is represented with the calm dignity associated with the work of Hall, a senior contributor to London's popular journal the *Graphic*. This extraordinary moment in the history of the Irish Parliamentary Party at Westminster has been discussed by historians in terms of the Irish MPs' well-organised plan of parliamentary obstruction over the previous days and the heated atmosphere created by the debates over coercion and the possibility of a general strike in Ireland against increased levels of rent. Hall focuses on the man himself, the new young MP for Tipperary. We see him slowly stepping on to the floor of the House, his hat in his right hand, his left hand jauntily in his trouser pocket. Years later, Dillon's old parliamentary colleague T.P. O'Connor would remember Dillon in his *Memoirs*, describing him in 1881 at the age of twenty-nine:

> He was a very striking addition to the figures on our benches, and for a time stood out almost from every other member of the House of Commons. Very tall, very thin, with a long, thin face. Coal black hair and eyes, he was another who looked rather like a Spanish than an Irish figure. Painters and sculptors and men of letters raved about the beauty of his face, and especially of his eyes. Henry Holloway, the great artist in mosaics, chose him for one of the saintly figures in the window he had to make for a church. George Meredith glows over his eyes in one of his letters.[2]

Many of the fascinating Irish people who feature in this book have benefited from such close personal attention. The Anglo-Irish interchange between such artists, politicians and poets as Daniel Maclise (see p.67), Charles Stewart Parnell (see p.48) and W.B. Yeats (see pp.17 and 37) has, on the whole, been well documented in biographies and historical studies. This book aims to bring them all together in order to explore, with the added benefit of visual evidence, their contribution to London intellectual life in the age of Queen Victoria. Viewers and readers are asked to equate the historical phenomenon of the individual with the visual product of the period. As with the example of John Dillon, we can check the biography against the image.

John Dillon Leaving the House of Commons
Sydney Prior Hall, 1881
Pencil and gouache on card, 420 x 313mm (16¹/₂ x 12³/₈")
National Gallery of Ireland

On 3 February 1881, John Dillon, MP for Tipperary (1851–1927), continually interrupted the Liberal Prime Minister, W.E. Gladstone, and after having been 'named' by the Speaker he was asked to leave the House. These interruptions, which were repeated by thirty-six members of the Irish Parliamentary Party, were caused by the Speaker's decision to terminate debate on the Protection of Person and Property (Ireland) Bill, in which Dillon had suggested that Irish farmers might resort to violence if evictions continued. Looking over the head of Gladstone's Cabinet colleague Joseph Chamberlain, we see Dillon leaving the opposition benches, while behind him a cheering John Redmond, whose first debate it was, waves his order papers in one hand and raises the other in a clenched-fist salute.

The names listed in the last paragraph suggest, not surprisingly, that the dominant intellectual contributors to Ireland's occupation of London in the nineteenth century were men. The role of Irishwomen in the spheres of art, politics and literature was obviously limited and is only now emerging into the mainstream of nineteenth-century studies.[3] The aim of the original exhibition and this book is to explore the totality of Irish intellectual contributions to Victorian London: in that context, it is vital that we address the question of the relationship between Irishwomen, artists and the representation of Ireland.

In attempting to do so, we do not always have access to the range of material necessary to allow such a straightforward equation as that between Sydney Prior Hall's heroic image of the defiant Irish MP and T.P. O'Connor's warm memories of a dead colleague. It is worth, on the one hand, looking at how visual artists allegorised Ireland, while, on the other, examining how Irish female models were represented by an assortment of Irish and non-Irish artists, most of whom were male but some of whom were female. Apart from refocusing attention on the artistic, literary and political contribution of the Irish to Victorian London, it is hoped to reclaim a number of forgotten individuals and groups, many of whom have been sidelined due to gender and/or lack of a distinctive voice.

Although literary figures who contributed actively to London intellectual life, such as Sydney Owenson (otherwise known as Lady Morgan), Caroline Norton and Anna Jameson feature in this study, the majority of the Irishwomen depicted here acted in more passive roles as muses to male artists. When we look at such a literary star as Owenson, it is not surprising to discover that in 1829 she personally commissioned a marble bust of herself in Paris from the celebrated French sculptor David d'Angers, (see p.27)[4] while Mrs Jameson, author of key Victorian texts on the explanation of religious art such as *Sacred and Legendary Art* (1848), was the subject of an early calotype by Hill and Adamson of the 1840s (see p.69). Focusing on recognisable and well-known female intellectuals, these portraits (rewarding as they are to record and to view) are a far cry from the relative anonymity characterising the representations of such Victorian Irishwomen in London as Joanna Hiffernan, Kathleen Newton (see p.71), Mary Ryan (see p.73), and most especially the spinners and embroiderers who were shipped over to sit on exhibition stands in 1888 in London's Olympia (see p.75). The Irish village at Olympia was a romantic creation, but the Ireland it showed to London was an active one peopled by the Kells Embroiderers, who made luxury objects for consumption at the heart of the empire. Irishwomen as much as Irishmen were ready to take on the practical side of the Union and exploit their talents.[5]

In 1842, the Cork-born artist Daniel Maclise exhibited *The Origin of the Harp* (see p.58) at London's Royal Academy. Resident in London some fifteen years, Maclise had been exhibiting annually at the Royal Academy since 1829 and was made a full Academician in 1840, the same year that he exhibited his celebrated portrait of his close friend Charles Dickens. His representation of an allegorical scene from the highly popular poems of his fellow countryman

Thomas Moore suggested a new seriousness in the occasional 'Irish' works that he had produced up until then. Previously, only a few of his paintings had proclaimed his Irish roots to the London audiences who viewed the annual Royal Academy exhibitions, at Somerset House until 1836 and then at the newly built National Gallery on Trafalgar Square (the Royal Academy did not move to Burlington House, Piccadilly, until 1867). These earlier Irish paintings had suggested a romantic fascination with violence or humour, as is the case with *Snap Apple Night or All Hallow's Eve in Ireland* of 1833 (private collection). Commenting on this particular painting, William Maginn (see p.26), the Cork-born editor of *Fraser's Magazine* (see p.27), had gone so far as to declare it a 'truly Irish picture', for as he pointed out, presumably for the amusement of his London readers, we see fortune-telling by the fire, conviviality and lots of drinking.[6] But now, in 1842, Irishness took on a different tone. The subject was historical and poetic; the genre-like elements of Maclise's Irish cottage interiors were no longer of interest. Instead, in turning to a subject from Moore's famed *Irish Melodies* (see p.31), Maclise was offering an allegorised representation of national myth and fulfilling the dual obligations of a true academician, to paint elevated subject matter while representing it through the medium of the idealised nude figure.

In *The Origin of the Harp*, a beautiful woman jilted by her lover stands at the water's edge, resigned to her fate. As Moore's poem suggests, her curvaceous form, her flowing locks of hair and the presence of some handy seaweed assist in her divinely inspired transformation into the melodious harp that had been a national symbol of Ireland since at least the seventeenth century. Moore is also remembering the genre of eighteenth-century Jacobite and nationalist *aislingí* (allegorical poetry), in which Ireland is a beautiful woman abandoned by her lover and awaiting deliverance.[7] The Royal Academy catalogue carried the appropriate lines from Moore's poem:

Still her bosom rose fair – still her cheek smil'd the same –
While her sea beauties gracefully form'd the light frame;
And her hair, as, let loose, o'er her white arm it fell,
Was chang'd to bright chords utt'ring melody's spell.[8]

Although depicting the creation of a musical instrument, Maclise's painting and of course Moore's poem are also about national origins. The essence of Ireland, as well as her music, suggested an ancient, heroic beauty. The act of transformation reminds us of an Ovidian tale of cultural origins, yet its northern location of grotto-like stalactites and a cold sea leading to a setting sun focuses attention on a North Atlantic world. In that non-Mediterranean ambience, Ireland had a legitimate history fully comparable to other tales of national beginnings that were current by the 1840s.

Two key things need to be emphasised when exploring the production of Maclise's painting based on Moore's poem. Both poem and painting were produced in London and both had English audiences in mind. As is also visible in Maclise's engraved illustrations to Moore's *Melodies*, the focus is on

The Origin of the Harp
Daniel Maclise, 1842
Oil on canvas, 1118 x
864mm (44 x 34")
Manchester City Galleries

This painting illustrates a poem by Thomas Moore (1779–1852) of the same name that had first appeared in his famous *Irish Melodies* and tells the story of an Irishwoman who, having been jilted by her lover, stands at the water's edge, resigned to her fate. Maclise's siren epitomises the popular representation of Celtic allegory in mid-nineteenth-century London. An engraved version of the painting appears in Maclise's illustrations to Moore's *Melodies*.

making Ireland understandable and acceptable to a wider population. The rejected siren in the *Harp* painting allegorises an ancient nation but one that by means of such a form of representation can stand proudly beside other European nations. Similarly, in his book illustrations, such as the page representing *The Harp That Once through Tara's Halls* (see p.31), Maclise focuses on a feudal yet highly civilised past when Ireland boasted kings and courts with harpists, beautiful maidens and brave knights.[9]

Although allegorised representations of Ireland in the guise of Erin or Hibernia had appeared prior to 1842 and Maclise's *The Origin of the Harp*, the exhibition at the Royal Academy of this elaborate national myth was the first major public display of such a type in nineteenth-century London. It was in fact to spawn a host of female depictions of Ireland that persisted into the early twentieth century. Ironically, unlike most of the subsequent personifications, the model for Maclise's 1842 painting was not Irish. As we will see, even within a few years of the *Harp* painting, and even for

Maclise himself, the sine qua non for this particular genre was to be the use of an authentic Irish model. This was to become especially true in London-based images of Ireland. But in 1842 the model for *The Origin of the Harp* was an Englishwoman. On a number of occasions between 1840 and 1842, Maclise joined Dickens on refreshing trips to the sea at Broadstairs in east Kent. While there they observed the 'charms', as they called them, of a woman they both referred to as 'the Screamer', possibly a Miss Strivens, who lived locally and enjoyed swimming. Dickens wrote to Maclise of the Screamer's 'swelling bosom', while Maclise, in a letter to his other great friend John Forster, confirmed his representation of the 'Irish nymph', as he called her, as the Screamer.[10]

By 1846, the choice of an English model to represent Ireland had changed dramatically. In turning to the well-known figure of Caroline Norton, a poet, novelist and granddaughter of Richard Brinsley Sheridan, Maclise found a most satisfying visualisation of an Irish ideal. Norton was of Irish origin, beautiful and intelligent. In Maclise's study of her as Erin, she thrusts her hip in a similarly sensuous manner to the marine siren in the earlier painting, but unlike that figure, Ireland now holds a harp as opposed to merely mimicking its shape. The representation of Norton was most probably a private study produced by Maclise while he worked on one of his most important commissions, the decoration of the newly built House of Lords in the Palace of Westminster. In 1846, the Fine Arts Commission requested Maclise to paint frescos of Chivalry and later one of Justice. The latter fresco, when completed, showed the idealised female figure standing between the two pillars of the Law as she holds a pair of scales. Maclise used the inspired choice of Norton as his model for Justice.[11] As suggested, Norton's full figure was a type that Maclise found attractive, but also she herself had suffered a great deal as the victim of marital and social injustice. Later in 1885, George Meredith would utilise Norton as a model for his heroine Diana of the Crossways, 'a lady', as he claimed in his prefatory note, 'of high distinction for wit and beauty, the daughter of an illustrious Irish House [who] came under the shadow of calumny'. In the novel, Diana has

> dark large eyes full on the brows; the proud line of a straight nose in right measure to the bow of the lips; reposeful red lips, shut, and their curve of the slumber-smile at the corners. Her forehead was broad; the chin of a sufficient firmness to sustain that noble square; the brows marked by a soft thick brush to the temples; her black hair plainly drawn along her head to the knot.[12]

The resemblance to Maclise's now rather damaged sketch of Norton as Erin is eerily uncanny. In the final representation of Norton as Justice in the House of Lords fresco, she exudes legal righteousness dressed in a suitably timeless gown and blue cloak. In the fresco she is flanked by angels and examples of justice done, while in the earlier transformation of her as Erin, even if only a sketch for a commissioned work representing Justice, Maclise softens the severity of her look, adds laurel leaves to her hair and balances the harp on the left with a piece of rolled paper on the right. Does the paper represent a petition, a request for Ireland then in the midst of famine?

The high-art female personification of Ireland that begins with Maclise is by no means limited to artists of Irish origin. For the rest of the century, English-based artists as diverse as Ford Madox Brown and Julia Margaret Cameron or the American James McNeill Whistler and the French artist James Tissot and eventually the Belfast-born John Lavery all participated in the representation of Irish models. For many years scholars have been analysing the popular representation of the female Erin or Hibernia in London-based illustrated journals. In a *Punch* cartoon such as *Hibernia Consolatrix*, drawn by John Tenniel (see p.44), which dates from 5 June 1886, Ireland is represented in the guise of a barefoot milkmaid who consoles the weary unhorsed knight, the Liberal Prime Minister, W.E. Gladstone, whose Irish Home Rule Bill would be defeated three days later. Although Ireland herself is usually seen, as here, as young and ostensibly innocent, she is more frequently juxtaposed with a simianised male figure who represents the Irish viewed by England as brutal, aggressive or, by contrast, doltish, uneducated and peasant-dominated.[13]

A very different image of Ireland is offered in what we might call the fine-art representation of Ireland. In examining the painted, engraved or photographed image, we encounter a different world. Ireland, with Maclise and his late-Victorian successors, is represented in a mode driven less by prejudice and more by contemporary realities. We meet a range of women, not a single type. Instead of Tenniel's virginal Hibernian companion to sturdy Britannia, in time we meet the streetwise modern woman.

In his *Autobiography and Reminiscences*, first published in the 1880s, the artist William Powell Frith recalled an encounter he had had thirty years earlier with an Irishwoman on Albany Street off Regent's Park. The woman was an orange seller, a common employment of recent emigrants from Ireland. Frith tells us that she boasted 'a rare type of rustic beauty', and that he invited her to pose for him. A painting resulted from the encounter which is today in the collection of the Royal Academy.

> Her smile as she offered her oranges was very bewitching, and had no doubt assisted her in creating a taste for oranges on many occasions. I became a large purchaser, and succeeded, after much trouble, in getting her to promise to sit for me, provided I would go to her confessor (she was Irish and a Catholic), and get his consent ... I determined to paint a laughing face from her – under the most favourable conditions a most difficult thing to do, but in her case hopeless, unless I could have induced her to go on for two hours selling imaginary oranges to phantom purchasers.[14]

With artist and model finally ensconced in Frith's studio in Notting Hill, conversation between the Irish orange seller and the artist of *Derby Day* soon began to flag and after a while the model fell asleep. Frith quickly abandoned 'the laughing subject and painted *The Sleepy Model*', who, he writes, 'now sleeps all day long in the Diploma Gallery [of the Royal Academy]'.[15]

Within a few years of Frith's painting of a sleeping Irish fruit seller, Henry Mayhew's exhaustive study of the London poor would highlight the Irish penchant for street vending in the capital.[16] Contemporaneous with Mayhew's findings is Ford Madox Brown's beautiful painting of *The Irish Girl* of 1860 (see p.72). This too is a portrait of an orange seller 'from the sister isle', as Brown's first biographer, Ford Madox Hueffer, was to write years later.[17] In 1856, Brown came across the Irish girl during his search for Irish models for his great painting *Work*, which he laboured on throughout the 1850s. The finished portrait of *The Irish Girl*, which Brown exhibited separately in London in 1860, was never actually included in *Work* and he changed her from an orange seller to a girl holding a cornflower, a symbol of celibacy and delicacy. In his diary, Brown writes of the research he carried out to find the right models for the Irish inclusions in *Work*, explaining how he

> went into Gray's Inn Lane to look for Irish people & after some prowling about found a poor woman & baby in Holborn who next day brought me a young man & [in] six days I painted these 3 into the picture pretty satisfactorily although I can scarce make sure of what I am about as yet.[18]

In recent years, research by Gerard Curtis, Joel Hollander and others has emphasised the Irish dimension to Brown's *Work*. Painted in the artist's London home in Kentish Town as he prepared *Work*, *The Irish Girl* is an intense study of a London experience that contrasts with the generalised study of the bad treatment meted out to another orange seller in the background of *Work*, whose trade is disturbed by a policeman.[19] As John Lavery's 1890 painting of yet another *Irish Girl* demonstrates (see p.74), street sellers would continue until the end of the century as an acceptable trope for representing Irishwomen in London. The irony here is that the sitter, whom Lavery met when she was a flowergirl on Regent Street and later married, turned out to be most probably Welsh.[20]

Irishwomen models were no different from any other ethnic group in later nineteenth-century London when it came to their exploitation by male artists. We have noticed Frith's casual and, for his purposes, advantageous use of an anonymous orange seller. Yet, when we turn to artists such as Whistler and Tissot and explore their relationships with and representations of Irishwomen who happened to be both mistresses and constant models, new possibilities for the Irish female emigrant begin to emerge.

James McNeill Whistler's relationship with Joanna Hiffernan has been well documented. Born around 1843 in Ireland, she met Whistler in 1860 and lived with him until at least 1866. She is the model for such well-known works as *Symphony in White, No. 1, The White Girl* of 1862 in the National Gallery of Art in Washington, DC, and Tate's *Symphony in White, No. 2, Little White Girl* of 1864 (Royal Academy, 1865). In *Weary* (see p.71), an etching of 1863, Whistler represents Hiffernan resting, her famous 'copper-coloured hair' spread out across the back of the armchair. Hiffernan has been much discussed in the Whistler literature as the most exciting of his mistresses-cum-muses.[21] To the Pennells, early biographers of Whistler in 1908, 'Joe', as she is frequently called, is described as 'Irish, Roman Catholic ... a woman of next to no education, but of keen intelligence'.[22] Her hair inspired, we are told, not only the American artist, who claimed that it was 'like everything Venetian one had dreamed of', but also his friend Gustave Courbet, who in 1865 was to paint her at least four times as *La Belle Irlandaise*. In Courbet's composition, Hiffernan admires herself in a hand mirror and combs her tresses with her hand.[23] In a letter of 1863, George Du Maurier, then a caricaturist and in time the author of *Trilby* (1894), the story of a half-Irish Parisian model, described Hiffernan as 'fiery' and wrote of how she was the cause of fierce jealousy on the part of Whistler.[24] As Elizabeth Prettejohn has carefully argued, later accounts of Whistler, right up to the large exhibition at the Tate Gallery, London, in 1994, have maintained this caricature of the Irish model as a racy, 'effervescent personality'.[25] The fact that Whistler portrays her in *Weary* as a relaxed and detached individual is rarely commented upon. Instead, in keeping with the tenor of a century of observation on Hiffernan's relationship with the male artist, the 1994 Tate Gallery catalogue goes so far as to say that, in the etching *Weary*, 'with her beauty, the glossy texture of her dress and hair, she was voluptuous and tempting, a Danaë newly awakened'.[26] In opposition to that viewpoint, it could be argued that what is happening here is that Hiffernan, an Irish woman posing in Whistler's Chelsea studio, is participating in a modernist experiment that tested the boundaries between portraiture and subject scenes. In February 1862, Du Maurier wrote of how Joanna Hiffernan came to visit him with Whistler, 'got up like a duchess, without crinoline – the mere *making up* of her bonnet by Madame somebody or other in Paris had cost 50 fr.'[27] Here, Du Maurier is aghast at the fact that Hiffernan was dressing above her station and also extravagantly. In mentioning this fact, he articulates the fate of many Irishwomen who are now remembered only as artists' models; class mobility was a possible outcome of their modest fame.

A decade after the incident described by Du Maurier, Kathleen Newton, née Kelly, the product of an Irish Catholic upbringing, travelled to India to marry a surgeon in the Indian Civil Service but soon divorced on grounds of adultery and eventually settled in a north London suburb with the London-based French artist James Tissot. This artist's extraordinary series of paintings and prints of his short love affair with Kathleen (she died of consumption at the age of twenty-eight) is one of the most touching accounts of an Irishwoman's representation in Victorian art.[28] Equally, Julia Margaret Cameron's compelling photographs of the former Irish beggar girl Mary Ryan, produced in the 1860s, show the transformation of an exiled vagrant into an angelic beauty (see p.73). It was while viewing photographs of Ryan that Henry Cotton, a rising official in the Bengal Civil Service and an advanced Liberal, spied his future wife and duly asked Mrs Cameron for the hand of her employee. Within a few years Mary Ryan was to become Lady Cotton, wife of the Chief Commissioner of Assam and a leading member of the Anglo-Indian elite.[29]

In an 1878 etching, Tissot represented Kathleen Newton as *Printemps* ('Spring'; see p.71), which was exhibited that same year at the fashionable and progressive Grosvenor Gallery in London. In the print, and in line with Du Maurier's comment on Joe Hiffernan, Newton is elaborately presented in a light muslin dress with an abundance of ribbons. The location is the garden of the home that Newton and Tissot shared at Grove End Road in St John's Wood. With its long slender shape, the print of Newton is comparable to a contemporary fashion plate. This tall, narrow format was, by 1878, highly fashionable both in advertising and in the Aesthetic Movement's delight in Japanese pillar prints.[30] In one of his most famous representations of his mistress, *Mavourneen* of 1877, Tissot emphasised her beauty; one biographer of Tissot referred to Newton as the '*ravissante Irlandaise*'. In *Mavourneen*, the artist also stressed her sartorial elegance and her ethnic origins and recalled the highly popular yet melancholic Victorian song:

> Kathleen Mavourneen! The grey dawn is breaking,
> The horn of the hunter is heard on the hill;
> The lark from her light wing the bright dew is shaking, –
> Kathleen Mavourneen! What, slumbering still?[31]

In Tissot's work, the convent-educated Kathleen Newton is represented as an always immaculately dressed suburb dweller, sauntering around her London garden. This slim, modern woman with her Japanese fan, appearing in what the *Daily Telegraph* of 1879 called a picture 'of the "detached villa" kind' suggests, as Nancy Marshall has pointed out, the 'potentially pleasurable ambiguity of female chastity'.[32] At the same time, Tissot's image of Newton posits a very different role for the modern Irishwoman when compared with *Punch*'s acquiescent Hibernia, of only a few years later, coming to the aid of the weary Gladstone in 1886 (see p.44).

The exhibition of photographs by Julia Margaret Cameron that Henry Cotton viewed in 1865 at the French Gallery in London included many images of a young Irish girl whom Mrs Cameron had first encountered in 1859 begging with her mother on Putney Heath. The photographer took her in and gave her a job in her household. By 1865–7, Ryan was posing continually for Mrs Cameron – as demonstrated in *The Irish Immigrant* of 1865–6 (see p.73). Here, Ryan wears a long-sleeved white gown that also appears in a host of other photographs of the time; in some she is *A Flower of Paradise*, while in others she is *After the Manner of Perugino* or *Francia*, two fifteenth-century Italian artists particularly associated, in mid-Victorian taste, with the representation of angels.[33] But by 1867, the same year as her marriage, Mary Ryan was posing as *The Gardener's Daughter*, an image based on Tennyson's poem of the same name:

One arm aloft —

Gown'd in pure white, that fitted to the shape —
Holding the bush, to fix it back, she stood,
A single stream of all her soft brown hair
Pour'd on one side:

This use of Mary Ryan to illustrate a poem by the Poet Laureate is quite a dramatic turn of events for the daughter of recent emigrants from Limerick. Within the same year, the Tennysons would attend Ryan's marriage to Henry Cotton, while their son acted as a page.[34] But before all that happened the photographer did not necessarily allow her admiration for the beauty and aesthetic potential of her favourites to colour her attitudes to their rank. Ryan was usually requested to ride outside Mrs Cameron's carriage, as other servants did. Indeed, in 1864, Mrs Cameron ironically inscribed a photo of Ryan as 'My beggar-maid, now 15!' invoking Tennyson's poem of a similar title.[35] Housemaids such as Ryan may have been offered exceptional opportunities in the Cameron establishment, but they always knew their place. A recent examination of the pricing of Mrs Cameron's photographs also shows that images of such models were never valued as highly as those of the national celebrities who sat for the photographer. In 1868, an image of the Poet Laureate could fetch 16 shillings or 21 shillings if autographed, while an image of Mary Ryan might reach only 5 shillings.[36]

As is clear from the various examples cited, the representation of Irishwomen in London between the 1840s and the 1870s was varied. It should be pointed out that none of those Irishwomen discussed were in fact professional models, although some decades later the names of a number of Irishwomen appear in the account books of the Royal Academy as official models.[37] As such the majority of Irish models possibly fitted into Oscar Wilde's 1889 definition as it appeared in a rather breezy article on the subject in the *English Illustrated Magazine*:

As a rule the model, nowadays, is a pretty girl, from about twelve to twenty-five years of age, who knows nothing about art, cares less, and is merely anxious to earn seven or eight shillings a day without much trouble.[38]

The difference between Wilde's characterisation of models and the women considered here — Joanna Hiffernan, Kathleen Newton and Mary Ryan — is that the individual personalities of each of these three women seriously contributed to the making of the prints and photographs discussed. In other words, in the creation of the images of these women, an elision has taken place between the supposed difference between portraiture and subject pictures. The various nineteenth-century representations of Irishwomen analysed in this essay show a movement from national allegory to modern woman and even if, for example, Tissot represents his mistress as *Printemps*, the point is that it is still a picture of Kathleen Newton, an Irish émigrée in nineteenth-century London, and that knowledge creates part of its impact. This contribution by an interesting group of Irishwomen to the making and meaning of a range of pictures in Victorian England is a previously unacknowledged contribution to British intellectual life.

NOTES

1 Lyons (1968), p.44. Although Hall's drawing of Dillon's suspension was not represented in the *Graphic*, Parnell's removal did appear (although not drawn by Hall) on 12 February 1881, p.156.
2 O'Connor (1929), Vol.I, pp.139–40. In 1887, Meredith wrote of Dillon's eyes, 'They are the most beautiful I have ever beheld in a head – clear deep wells with honesty at bottom': Cline (1970), Vol.II, p.858.
3 Owenson (2000); Bourke et al. (2002).
4 Owenson (1830), Vol.I, p.309.
5 Helland, forthcoming.
6 Weston (2001), p.72; for Maclise's career, see also Arts Council (1972).
7 Thuente (1994), pp.50–55, 175–6; Dunne (1988), p.87.
8 Graves (1906), Vol.V, p.154.
9 Maclise's *The Origin of the Harp* illustration appears in Moore (1846), no.88; see also Turpin (1985).
10 Dickens to Maclise, 14 August 1842, House, et al. (1974), p.308; Maclise to Forster, Victoria & Albert Museum, London, National Art Library, MS48.E.19, April 1842, no.15; Weston (2001), p.116.
11 Arts Council (1972), pp.84–9, especially no.96; see Weston (2001), Ch.6, for the background to Norton and the House of Lords commission. For Norton herself, see Acland (1948), Chedzoy (1992) and Dolin (2002).
12 Meredith (1910), pp.104–5.
13 The key work on Victorian caricature is still Curtis (1997).
14 Frith (1888), Vol.I, p.166.
15 Frith (1888), Vol.I, pp.166–7. See also Postle and Vaughan (1999), pp.56, 66.
16 See especially the representation of the orange seller in Mayhew (1861), Vol.I, p.97. For comment see Barringer (1994), Vol.I, pp.267–8; Cullen (1997), p.139. See also Jacqueline Turton's 'Mayhew's Irish: The Irish Poor in Mid Nineteenth-century London', in Swift and Gilley (1999), pp.122–55.
17 Hueffer (1896), p.168; see also Cullen (1997), p.140.
18 Surtees (1981), p.194, entry for 16 March 1857.
19 Curtis (2002), pp.67–96; Hollander (1997); Cullen (1997), pp.135–42.
20 Lavery (1940), pp.65–6.
21 Jiminez (2001), pp.275–8; MacDonald et al. (2003), pp.76–91.
22 Pennell (1908), Vol.I, pp.94–5.
23 The reference to Venetian hair is in Dorment et al. (1994), p.74; for Courbet's various paintings of Hiffernan, see Faunce and Nochlin (1988), pp.162–6.
24 Du Maurier (1951), p.219.
25 Prettejohn (1996), p.303, quoting Dorment et al. (1994), p.75.
26 Dorment et al. (1994), p.82.
27 Du Maurier (1951), p.105.
28 Jimenez (2001), pp.397–400.
29 For Ryan's biography see Wolf (1998), p.226 (research by Stephanie Lipscomb) and Olsen (2003), Ch.8; for Henry Cotton see Edward C. Moulton's entry in the *Oxford Dictionary of National Biography* (2004), Vol.13, p.611.
30 Wentworth (1978), pp.154–7.
31 Phrase coined by Marita Ross, see Brooke (1968). For the Mavourneen (trans: 'my darling') print, see Wentworth (1978), pp.142–3. The song was written by the American, Louisa Macartney Crawford (possibly in the 1830s) and set to music by Frederick William Nicholls Crouch; for words and music see/listen to http://freepages.music.rootsweb.com/~edgmon/stkathleen.htm (accessed on 19 July 2004).
32 Marshall (1999), pp.33, 41.
33 Cox and Ford (2003), pp.256–7.
34 Olsen (2003), p.193. For *The Gardener's Daughter*, see Cox and Ford (2003), no.456, p.257.
35 Olsen (2003), pp.192–3. For *My beggar-maid*, see Cox and Ford (2003), p.124.
36 Wolf (1998), pp.212, 217.
37 Royal Academy of Arts, London, Archive TRE/7/1 Model Receipts, 1897–1902. Irishwomen such as Nellie Gilroy and May Sullivan sat regularly as models in the RA Schools and were paid 8 shillings per sitting.
38 Wilde (1889), p.313.

Visual arts

William Mulready, 1786–1863
John Linnell, 1833
Oil on panel, 311 x 254mm (12¼ x 10")
National Portrait Gallery, London (NPG 1690)

Painted at the height of Mulready's career, this portrait of the Irish-born painter was exhibited at the Royal Academy of Arts in 1833. A childhood emigrant from County Clare, Mulready was made an Academician in 1818 and remained an active participant in RA affairs all his life. Such was his contemporaneous fame that William Makepeace Thackeray, in a *Fraser's Magazine* review of the 1839 RA exhibition, referred to the two key exhibitors as 'King Mulready' and 'Prince Maclise'. The fact that both were Irish indicates the extent of Irish infiltration of London artistic establishments.

Daniel Maclise, 1806–70
Edward Matthew Ward, 1846
Oil on panel, 457 x 352mm (18 x 13⁷/₈")
National Portrait Gallery, London (NPG 616)

Maclise was one of the most celebrated Irish artists based in London in the nineteenth century. By 1846, when this portrait was painted by his friend Ward, he had established himself as a history painter but one who also indulged in occasional works with Irish subject matter. By the end of the decade he would win the commission to paint frescos to decorate the newly built House of Lords.

CAROLINE NORTON, a study for the great fresco of Justice in the House of Lords. By Maclise

Erin
Daniel Maclise, c.1846
Oil on canvas, 1067 x 762mm (42 x 30")
Patrick Guinness

Here, the subject, model and artist are all Irish, and Maclise's choice of the brilliant and slightly scandalous Irish writer Caroline Norton (1808–77) to represent Erin or Ireland is in itself significant. Given her much-publicised separation from her husband, and her determination to earn her own living by her pen in the traditionally masculine world of political commentary, Norton represented independence of status as well as mind. Maclise's choice of this famous woman to personify the spirit of her country is central to the way Ireland was represented at this level of Victorian culture, very far from the themes of dependence or inferiority too often assumed to have been the norm.

Anna Brownell Jameson, 1794–1860
David Octavius Hill and Robert Adamson, 1843–8
Calotype, 203 x 137mm (8 x 5³/₈")
Scottish National Portrait Gallery, Edinburgh

Produced by two pioneers of early photography, this
portrait is of one of the most influential art critics of the
nineteenth century. Anna Murphy was the daughter of
an Irish artist of a nationalist persuasion who left Dublin
for England in the late 1790s. In 1825 she married an Irish
barrister, Robert Jameson, but the marriage was not a
success. As Mrs Jameson, she published her first art-
historical book in 1836 and her writings soon became
popular, because she explained a painting's original
purpose as well as citing its historical context. Her
discussion of religious art was particularly helpful to a
largely Protestant readership, baffled by the highly
Catholic subject matter of the Italian paintings increasingly
being purchased by London's National Gallery from the
1830s onwards. *Sacred and Legendary Art* (1848) is her
most celebrated book. As well as being a key figure in
foregrounding an Irish intellectual presence in London,
she is also an important early voice in explaining the
iconographic representation of women in historical art.

Caractacus
John Henry Foley, 1856
Plaster maquette, height 686mm (27")
Guildhall Art Gallery, Corporation of London

Irish sculptors fared well in London in the Victorian
period. In the 1860s no fewer than three Irishmen were
working on groups for the Albert Memorial. The most
celebrated was Foley, who was born in Dublin but went to
London in 1834 to join his elder brother and fellow
sculptor, Edward. In the mid-1850s Foley was
commissioned by the City of London to carve a colossal
marble of Caractacus, which, when completed in 1857, was
placed outside the Egyptian Hall in the Mansion House.
The smaller plaster maquette shows the Celtic king of
c.50 CE resolutely addressing his troops before a Roman
attack on the Welsh borders. Representing an early Briton
who troubled the Romans, the iconography is suitably
defiant in the face of an earlier empire, yet it represents
the work of a sculptor who – like many Irishmen –
benefited from working at the heart of the British Empire.

An Ejectment in Ireland (A Tear and a Prayer for Erin)
Robert George Kelly, 1847–8
Oil on canvas, 1168 x 1448mm (46 x 57")
Collection of Anthony J. Mourek on loan to the John J. Burns Library, Boston College

Exhibited at the British Institution in 1853, this painting aroused concern among the
London establishment regarding Irish political pictures on display in the metropolis.
As such the painting was, according to Walter Strickland, the authoritative author of
A Dictionary of Irish Artists (1913), 'actually discussed in the House of Commons'. Hansard
has not revealed any such discussion but the painting was reviewed in the pages of the
Illustrated London News (26 February 1853). It was criticised for both its 'vulgar' subject
matter and its artistic deficiencies, but the armed police restraining the farmer who has
tried to defend his home, while a priest calls on heaven as witness, makes a powerful
political point.

Weary
James McNeill Whistler, 1863
Etching and drypoint, 197 x 132mm (7³/₄ x 5¹/₄")
The British Museum, London

This print shows the Irishwoman Joanna Hiffernan
(b.1843), who in the 1860s acted as a model for both
Whistler (largely in London) and Gustave Courbet (in
France). For a number of years, Whistler and Hiffernan
lived together at 7a Queen's Road West, Chelsea, and
later at 7 Lindsey Row (now Cheyne Walk).

Printemps
James Tissot, 1878
Etching and drypoint,
381 x 135mm (15 x 5¹/₄")
The British Museum, London

The Irishwoman Kathleen Newton (née Kelly; 1854–82)
was the great love and inspiration of the French-born
artist James Jacques Tissot. This is one of a number of
Japanese-influenced prints in which she appears as a
season of the year and shows Newton in the garden of
the house she shared with the artist on Grove End
Road, St John's Wood.

The Irish Girl
Ford Madox Brown, 1860
Oil on canvas laid on board, 286 x 276mm (11¼ x 10⅞")
Yale Center for British Art, Paul Mellon Fund

In preparation for his great painting *Work* (1852?–65, Manchester City Galleries), Brown closely studied the Irish poor in London. Painted in his studio in Kentish Town, this portrait was sold by the artist for 40 guineas to the Leeds stockbroker Thomas Plint, who had earlier commissioned *Work*. In 1861 the painting was exhibited in London at the Hogarth Club, a private exhibiting society.

The Irish Immigrant
Julia Margaret Cameron, 1865–6
Albumen print, 322 x 262mm (12³/₄ x 10¹/₄")
The Royal Photographic Society Collection at the National Museum of Photography,
Film & Television

This photograph of a young woman in the guise of an Irish immigrant is one of many
such poses created by the pioneer photographer Julia Margaret Cameron to depict her
domestic servant the Irishwoman Mary Ryan (1848–1914).

An Irish Girl
John Lavery, 1890
Oil on canvas, 686 x 540mm (27 x 21¼")
Private collection

As he recounts in his autobiography, one day, while working in a friend's studio near Regent Street, Lavery saw 'a young girl with a bright red shawl round her head like a gypsy, in a neat navy-blue frock, standing under the Arches rather shyly holding a little basket of flowers that she was evidently offering for sale'. The girl told Lavery that she was Kathleen MacDermott and within a short time they were married. Although the portrait is entitled *An Irish Girl*, Lavery was later to discover that she was in fact Welsh and that her real name was Annie Evans.

THE EXHIBITS OF THE DONEGAL INDUSTRIAL FUND.

IRISH PEASANT WORKERS IN THEIR COTTAGES

Sketches at the Irish Exhibition
Wood engraving in *Queen*, 28 July 1888, p.109;
height 457mm (18")
The British Library

Founded in 1883 to aid Irish cottage industries, the Donegal Industrial Fund was particularly driven by the efforts of Alice Hart. In 1888, together with the Earl of Leitrim, Hart oversaw the creation of an Irish Exhibition at Olympia, London. The exhibition consisted of twelve thatched cottages occupied in some cases by women trained by Hart herself. Shown here are two tiers of sketches from the exhibition as illustrated in *Queen, or the Ladies Newspaper*, which gave good coverage to the event. In the upper image, two young women are shown at work on luxurious objects in the Kells Embroiderers' Cottage. Below, four vignettes display a Limerick lacemaker, a silver stitch embroiderer, the art of plant dyeing and the use of spinning wheels. These images from a popular women's magazine show how the Irish world, both idealised and exoticised, was presented to the English market.

Bibliography

Acland, Alice, *Caroline Norton* (Constable, London, 1948)

Arts Council of Great Britain, *Daniel Maclise 1806–1870* (exh. cat., National Portrait Gallery, London, and National Gallery of Ireland, Dublin, 1972)

Barringer, T.J. 'Representations of Labour in British Visual Culture, 1850–1875', 2 vols, University of Sussex, 1994 (unpublished dissertation)

Belford, Barbara, *Bram Stoker: A Biography of the Author of Dracula* (Weidenfeld and Nicolson, London, 1996)

Bourke, Angela et al. (eds), *The Field Day Anthology of Irish Writing*, Vols 4 and 5, *Irish Women's Writing and Traditions* (Cork University Press, Cork, 2002)

Boyce, D. George, and O'Day, Alan (eds), *Ireland in Transition, 1867–1921* (Routledge, London, 2004)

Brooke, Davis S., 'James Tissot and the "ravissante Irlandaise"', *Connoisseur*, May 1968, pp.55–9

Butler, Lady [Elizabeth], *An Autobiography* (Constable and Co., London, 1922)

Cave, Richard Allen, 'Staging the Irishman', in *Acts of Supremacy. The British Empire and the Stage, 1790–1930*, ed. J.S. Bratton, (Manchester University Press, Manchester, 1991), pp.62–128

Chedzoy, Alan, *A Scandalous Woman: The Story of Caroline Norton* (Allison and Busby, London, 1992)

Cline, C.L. (ed.), *The Letters of George Meredith*, 3 vols (Clarendon Press, Oxford, 1970)

Cox, Julian, and Ford, Colin (eds), *Julia Margaret Cameron: The Complete Photographs* (Thames and Hudson, London, 2003)

Cullen, Fintan, and Murphy, William M., *The Drawings of John Butler Yeats* (exh. cat., Albany Institute of History & Art, Albany, 1987)

—, *Visual Politics: The Representation of Ireland 1750–1930* (Cork University Press, Cork, 1997)

—, *The Irish Face: Redefining the Irish Portrait* (National Portrait Gallery, London, 2004)

Curtis, Gerard, *Visual Words: Art and the Material Book in Victorian England* (Ashgate, Aldershot, 2002)

Curtis, L. Perry, Jr, *Apes and Angels: The Irishman in Victorian Caricature* (rev. edn, Smithsonian Institution, Washington, DC, and London, 1997)

—, '"The Land for the People": Post-Famine Images of Eviction', in *Éire/Land*, ed. Vera Kreilkamp (exh. cat., McMullen Museum of Art, Boston College University of Chicago Press, Chicago, 2003), pp.85–92

Davis, Graham, *The Irish in Britain 1815–1914* (Gill and Macmillan, Dublin, 1991)

Deane, Seamus (ed.), *The Field Day Anthology of Irish Writing*, 3 vols (Field Day Publications, Derry, 1991)

Dolin, Kieran, 'The transfigurations of Caroline Norton', *Victorian Literature and Culture*, 30: 2, 2002, pp.503–27

Dorment, Richard, MacDonald, Margaret F., et al., *James McNeill Whistler* (Tate Gallery, London, 1994)

Downey, Edmund, *Twenty Years Ago* (Hurst and Blackett, London, 1905)

Du Maurier, Daphne (ed.), *The Young George Du Maurier: A Selection of His Letters, 1860–67* (Peter Davies, London, 1951)

Dunne, Tom, 'Haunted by History: Irish Romantic writing 1800–50', in *Romanticism in National Context*, Roy Porter and Mikuláš Teich (eds) (Cambridge University Press, Cambridge, 1988)

Edwards, Owen Dudley, and Storey, Patricia, 'The Irish Press in Victorian Britain', in *The Irish in the Victorian City*, ed. Roger Swift and Sheridan Gilley (Croom Helm, London, 1985), pp.158–78

Ellmann, Richard, *Oscar Wilde* (Hamish Hamilton, London, 1987)

Faunce, Sarah, and Nochlin, Linda, *Courbet Reconsidered* (Yale University Press, New Haven and London, 1988)

Fawkes, Richard, *Dion Boucicault: A Biography* (Quartet Books, London, 1979)

Fitzpatrick, David, 'A Curious Middle Place: The Irish in Britain, 1871–1921', in *The Irish in Britain 1815–1939*, ed. Roger Swift and Sheridan Gilley (Pinter Publishers, London, 1989), pp.10–59

Foster, R.F., *Paddy and Mr Punch: Connections in Irish and English History* (Allen Lane Penguin Press, London, 1993)

—, *W.B. Yeats: A Life*, Vol.1, *The Apprentice Mage, 1865–1914* (Oxford University Press, Oxford, 1997)

—, *The Irish Story: Telling Tales and Making It Up in Ireland* (Allen Lane Penguin Press, London, 2001)

Foster, Sally E., 'Irish wrong: Samuel Lover and the stage-Irishman', *Éire-Ireland*, 4, 1978, pp.34–45

Frayne, John P. (ed.), *Uncollected Prose by W.B. Yeats*, Vol.I, *First Reviews and Articles, 1886–1896* (Macmillan, London, 1970); with Colton Johnson, Vol.II, *1897–1939* (Macmillan, London, 1975)

Frazier, Adrian, *George Moore 1852–1933* (Yale University Press, New Haven and London, 2000)

Frith, W.P., *My Autobiography and Reminiscences*, 2 vols (Richard Bentley and Son, London, 1888)

Gilley, Sheridan, 'English Attitudes to the Irish in England', in *Immigrants and Minorities in British Society*, ed. Colin Holmes (Croom Helm, London, 1978), pp.81–110

Glendinning, Victoria, *Trollope* (Hutchinson, London, 1991)

Goldman, Paul, *Victorian Illustrated Books 1850–1870: The Heyday of Wood-Engraving* (British Museum, London, 1994)

Gould, Warwick, and Chapman, Wayne (eds), *Yeats Annual*, Vol.15, *A Special Number: Yeats and His Collaborators* (Palgrave Macmillan, London, 2002)

Graves, Algernon, *The Royal Academy of Arts: A Complete Dictionary of Contributors and Their Work from Its Foundation in 1769 to 1904*, 8 vols (Henry Graves & Co. Ltd and George Bell & Sons, London, 1906)

Gray, Peter (ed.), *Victoria's Ireland? Irishness and Britishness, 1837–1901* (Four Courts Press, Dublin, 2004)

Hall, Anna Maria, *Light and Shadows of Irish Life*, 3 vols (Garland Publishing, New York, 1973)

Hall, N. John, *Trollope and His Illustrators* (Macmillan, London, 1980)

Helland, Janice, 'Exhibiting Ireland: the Donegal Industrial Fund in London and Chicago', *Revue d'art canadienne/Canadian Art Review (RACAR)*, forthcoming

Hickman, Mary, 'Alternative Historiographies of the Irish in Britain: A Critique of the Segregation/Assimilation Model', in *The Irish in Victorian Britain: The Local Dimension*, ed. Roger Swift and Sheridan Gilley (Four Courts Press, Dublin, 1999), pp.236–53

Hollander, Joel A., 'Ford Madox Brown's *Work* (1865): the Irish Question, Carlyle, and the Great Famine', *New Hibernian Review*, 1: 1, 1997, pp.100–19

Holmes, Colin (ed.), *Immigrants and Minorities in British Society* (Croom Helm, London, 1978)

Holroyd, Michael, *Bernard Shaw*, Vol.I, *1856–1898: The Search for Love*; Vol.II, *1898–1918: The Pursuit of Power* (Chatto and Windus, London, 1988, 1989)

House, M., Storey, G., and Tillotson, K. (eds), *The Letters of Charles Dickens*, Vol.3 (Oxford University Press, Oxford, 1974)

Hueffer, Ford M., *Ford Madox Brown: A Record of His Life and Work* (Longmans, Green & Co., London, 1896)

Hutton, Clare (ed.), 'Francis Fahy's "Ireland in London: Reminiscences" (1921)', in *Yeats Annual*, Vol.15, *A Special Number: Yeats and His Collaborators*, ed. Warwick Gould and Wayne Chapman (Palgrave Macmillan, London, 2002), pp.233–80

Jimenez, Jill Berk (ed.), *Dictionary of Artists' Models* (Fitzroy Dearborn Publishers, London and Chicago, 2001)

Kelly, J.S., and Domville, Eric (eds), *The Collected Letters of W.B. Yeats*, Vol. I, *1865–1895* (Clarendon Press, Oxford, 1986)

Kreilkamp, Vera (ed.), *Éire/Land* (exh. cat., McMullen Museum of Art, Boston College, University of Chicago Press, Chicago, 2003)

Lavery, John, *The Life of a Painter* (Cassell and Co. Ltd, London, 1940)

Leerssen, Joep, *Mere Irish and Fíor-Ghael: Studies in the Idea of Irish Nationality, Its Development and Literary Expression Prior to the Nineteenth-Century* (Cork University Press, Cork, 1996)

Lyons, F.S.L., *John Dillon: A Biography* (Routledge and Kegan Paul, London, 1968)

McConkey, Kenneth, *Sir John Lavery RA, 1856–1941* (exh. cat., Ulster Museum, Belfast and Fine Art Society, London, 1984)

McCord, James N., 'The Image in England: The Cartoons of HB', in *Daniel O'Connell, Political Pioneer*, ed. Maurice O'Connell (Institute of Public Administration, Dublin, 1991), pp.57–71

McCormack, W.J., *Sheridan Le Fanu and Victorian Ireland* (Oxford University Press, Oxford, 1980)

McCormack, Jerusha (ed.), *Wilde the Irishman* (Yale University Press, New Haven and London, 1998)

MacDonald, Margaret F., Galassi, Susan Grace, and Ribeiro, Aileen, with Patricia de Montfort, *Whistler, Women, and Fashion* (Yale University Press, New Haven and London, 2003)

MacRaild, Donald, *Irish Migrants in Modern Britain 1750–1922* (Macmillan, London, 1999)

Marshall, Catherine, 'Painting Irish history: the famine', *History Ireland*, 4: 2, Autumn 1996, pp.46–50

Marshall, Nancy Rose, 'Image or Identity: Kathleen Newton and the London Pictures of James Tissot', in *Seductive Surfaces: The Art of Tissot*, ed. Kathleen Lochnan (Yale University Press, New Haven and London, 1999), pp.23–52

Mayhew, Henry, *London Labour and the London Poor*, 4 vols (London, 1861)

Meredith, George, *Diana of the Crossways* (Memorial Edition, Vol. XVI, Charles Scribner's Sons, New York, 1910)

Moore, Thomas, *Irish Melodies* (Longman, Brown, Green, and Longman's, London, 1846)

Murphy, William M., *Prodigal Father: The Life of John Butler Yeats (1839–1922)* (Cornell University Press, Ithaca and London, 1978)

Murray, Paul, *From the Shadow of Dracula: a life of Bram Stoker* (Jonathan Cape, London, 2004)

Nelson, James Malcolm, 'From Rory and Paddy to Boucicault's Myles, Shaun and Conn: the Irishman on the London stage, 1830–1860',

Éire-Ireland, 13, 1978, pp.79–105

O'Connor, T.P., *The Parnell Movement* (Kegan Paul, London, 1886)

—, *Memoirs of an Old Parliamentarian*, 2 vols (Ernest Benn Ltd, London, 1929)

O'Day, Alan, *The English Face of Irish Nationalism: Parnellite Involvement in British Politics 1880–1886* (Gill and Macmillan, Dublin, 1977)

—, 'Varieties of Anti-Irish Behaviour in Britain 1846–1922', in *Radical Violence in Britain 1840–1950*, ed. P. Panayi (Leicester University Press, London and Leicester, 1993), pp.26–43

O'Day, Alan (ed.), *A Survey of the Irish in England (1872): Hugh Heinrick* (Hambledon Press, London and Ronceverte, West Virginia, 1990)

O'Donnell, Frank Hugh, *History of the Irish Parliamentary Party*, 2 vols (Longmans and Co., London, 1910)

Olsen, Victoria, *From Life: Julia Margaret Cameron and Victorian Photography* (Aurum Press, London, 2003)

Ormond, Richard, *National Portrait Gallery: Early Victorian Portraits*, 2 vols (HMSO, London, 1973)

O'Sullivan, Patrick (ed.), *The Irish World Wide: History, Heritage, Identity*, 6 vols (Leicester University Press, Leicester and London, Vols 1 and 2, 1992; Vols 3–6, 1993)

Oxford Dictionary of National Biography, H.C.G. Matthew and Brian Harrison (eds), 60 vols (Oxford Universtiy Press, Oxford, 2004)

Owenson, Sydney, Lady Morgan, *France in 1829–30*, 2 vols (Saunders and Otley, London, 1830)

—, *The Wild Irish Girl: A National Tale*, ed. Claire Connolly and Stephen Copley (Pickering and Chatto, London, 2000)

Panayi, P. (ed.), *Radical Violence in Britain 1840–1950* (Leicester University Press, London and Leicester, 1993)

Pennell, E.R. and J., *The Life of James McNeill Whistler*, 2 vols (London and Philadelphia, 1908)

Petuchowski, Elizabeth, 'Mr Punch and Daniel O'Connell', *Éire-Ireland*, VII: 4, Winter 1972, pp.12–31

Postle, Martin, and Vaughan, William, *The Artist's Model from Etty to Spencer* (Merrell Holberton, London, 1999)

Prettejohn, Elizabeth, 'Locked in the myth', *Art History*, 19: 2, 1996, pp.301–7

—, *The Art of the Pre-Raphaelites* (Tate Publishing, London, 2000)

Pyle, Hilary, *The Different Worlds of Jack B. Yeats: His Cartoons and Illustrations* (Irish Academic Press, Dublin, 1994)

Shaw, Bernard, *Collected Letters, 1898–1910*, ed. Dan H. Laurence (Max Reinhardt, London, 1972)

Shaw, George Bernard, *The Matter with Ireland*, ed. Dan H. Laurence and David H. Greene (University of Florida Press, Gainesville, 2001)

Sheehy, Ian, 'Irish Journalists and

Litterateurs in Late Victorian London c.1870–1910', University of Oxford, 2003 (unpublished dissertation)

—, 'T.P. O'Connor and the Star, 1886–90', in *Ireland in Transition, 1867–1921*, ed. D. George Boyce and Alan O'Day (Routledge, London, 2004), pp.76–91

Stewart, Bruce (ed.), *Hearts and Minds: Irish Culture and Society under the Act of Union* (Colin Smythe, Gerrards Cross, 2002)

Strickland, Walter, *A Dictionary of Irish Artists*, 2 vols (Maunsel & Co., Dublin and London, 1913)

Surtees, Virginia (ed.), *The Diary of Ford Madox Brown* (Yale University Press, New Haven and London, 1981)

Swift, Roger, and Gilley, Sheridan (eds), *The Irish in the Victorian City* (Croom Helm, London, 1985)

—, *The Irish in Britain 1815–1939* (Pinter Publishers, London, 1989)

—, *The Irish in Victorian Britain: The Local Dimension* (Four Courts Press, Dublin, 1999)

Thorpe, James, *English Illustration: The Nineties* (Hacker Art Books, New York, 1975)

Thrall, Miriam M.H., *Rebellious Fraser's: Nol Yorke's Magazine in the Days of Maginn, Thackeray, and Carlyle* (Columbia University Press, New York, 1934)

Thuente, Mary Helen, *The Harp Re-strung: The United Irishmen and the Rise of Irish Literary Nationalism* (University of Syracuse Press, Syracuse, 1994)

Toomey, Deirdre, 'The Story-Teller at Fault: Oscar Wilde and Irish Orality', in *Wilde the Irishman*, ed. Jerusha McCormack (Yale University Press, New Haven and London, 1998), pp.24–35

Turpin, John, 'Maclise as a Book Illustrator', *Irish Arts Review*, 2: 2, 1985, pp.23–7

Vanity Fair: An Exhibition of Original Cartoons (exh. cat., National Portrait Gallery, London, 1976)

Wentworth, Michael Justin, *James Tissot: Catalogue Raisonné of His Prints* (Minneapolis Institute of Arts, Minneapolis, 1978)

Weston, Nancy, *Daniel Maclise: Irish Artist in Victorian London* (Four Courts Press, Dublin, 2001)

Wilde, Oscar, 'London models', *English Illustrated Magazine*, 6: 64, 1889, pp.313–19

Wolf, Sylvia, *Julia Margaret Cameron's Women* (exh. cat., Frick Collection, New York, Yale University Press, New Haven and London, 1998)

Yeats, W.B., *Autobiographies* (Macmillan, London, 1955)

Index

Picture credits

Locations and lenders are given in the captions, and further acknowledgements are given below.